THE AUTHORITY
OF THE BELIEVER

The Authority of the Believer

John A. MacMillan

A spiritual warfare classic which includes
The Authority of the Intercessor and
Encounter with Darkness

WingSpread Publishers
Camp Hill, Pennsylvania

WingSpread Publishers

3825 Hartzdale Drive · Camp Hill, PA 17011
www.wingspreadpublishers.com

A division of Zur Ltd.

The Authority of the Believer
ISBN: 978-1-60066-083-2
LOC Control Number: 2007921653
© 1981 Revised edition by Zur Ltd.

Previously published by Christian Publications, Inc.
First Christian Publications Revised Edition 1981
First Christian Publications Trade Edition 1997
First WingSpread Publishers Edition 2007
Originally published as a series of articles in 1932

Unless otherwise indicated Scripture quotations are taken from
The Holy Bible: King James Version or are the
author's own paraphrase.

Quotations cited as "ASV" are from the
American Standard Version of the Bible.

Those cited "RV" are from the
Revised Standard Version of the Bible, © 1946, 1952, 1971 by
Division of Christian Education of the National Council of
Churches of Christ in the United States of America.

Contents

The Authority of the Believer

Encounter with Darkness

THE AUTHORITY
OF THE
BELIEVER

Foreword

Rev. J.A. MacMillan (1873-1956), the author of these classic writings on spiritual warfare, was a Canadian. He came to Christ early in life and by the time he was in his early twenties, had been made an elder in the Presbyterian Church. He organized his own printing business in Toronto, Ontario, Canada and operated it successfully until, at the age of forty-nine, God called him to China as a missionary. The Christian and Missionary Alliance sent J.A. MacMillan and his wife to South China to manage the Mission's printing operation. He was ordained to the ministry while on the field in 1923.

MacMillan's ministry in China demonstrated both his wisdom and capabilities as a leader. When leadership was needed for the floundering Mission in the Philippines, the Board of Managers sent MacMillan to Zamboanga City to oversee the work. Under his administration the Mission was stabilized and the Ebenezer Bible School was opened to train nationals for the ministry. From 1926-1929 he ministered with great blessing in the Philippines.

His wife died in 1928; MacMillan and his small son returned to North America the following year. He served in deputation and administrative responsibilities until 1933 when he was appointed editor of adult curriculum for the publishing house. In 1934 he became assistant editor of *The Alliance Weekly* and was responsible for the editorial column for sixteen years.

Authority

When mountain walls confront the way.
Why sit and weep? Arise and say
"Be thou removed!" and they shall be
By the power of God cast in the sea.

All power on earth, all power in heaven,
To Christ, the Son of God, is given;
And from the throne He will endue,
And hindrances will flee from you.

O'er all the power of fiend and man
Say through the Lord, "I surely can";
Take from Him power on earth to tread
On serpent's sting, on dragon's head.

Whate'er thou art, O mountain high,
Where'er thou art, in earth or sky,
Whene'er thou art, truth is the same,
"Be thou removed, in Jesus name."

"Be thou removed!" Faith bids thee start
For yonder see—arise! depart!
I may, I can, I must, I will,
The purpose of my God fulfill.

Anonymous

Preface

The rapidly approaching end of the age is witnessing a tremendous increase in the activity of the powers of darkness. Unrest among the nations, more intense than at any previous time in earth's history, is due largely to the stirring up of the ambitions and passions of men, while the spread of an almost wholly secularized education is quietly doing away with the scriptural standards which formerly exerted a restraining influence among the so-called Christian peoples. Our wealth and social culture have not made us thankful to the Giver of all good, but have centered us upon the material things of the world, and have produced a self-sufficiency that quite ignores our dependence upon the Creator of all. Godlessness, which we have condemned so strongly in the Soviet Union, is almost equally as pronounced, though less blatant, in our own land.

These conditions are reacting strongly upon the great ministry of the Church of Christ, the giving of the gospel to the heathen world. War has closed many doors in foreign lands, and at the same time has cut off financial contributions in not a few countries which formerly took an active interest in missions. More serious still is the attitude of large sections of the Church toward the state of the heathen. No longer are these concerned about the lost souls which wander in darkness; their thought is centered on raising their social status and meeting their intellectual and physical needs. They seek, in their own jargon, to "build a better world," but the world they envision is one without a Savior. Christ, in their view, has degenerated into a Superman, an example which in their own feeble strength they seek to follow. To meet the situation, the Church of Christ needs a new conception of prayer. The urgent call is for men and women, wholly yielded to the Lord, whose eyes have been enlightened to see the ministry in the heavenlies to which they have been called. Such believers, whether as intercessors, or as workers at home, or missionaries on the foreign fields, may in union with the great Head of the Body, exercise an authority to which the powers of the air must give place wherever challenged.

The contents of this book first appeared as a series of articles in *The Alliance Weekly* (now *Alliance Life*). The first series appeared under the title *The Authority of the Believer*. A second series carried the title *The Authority of the Intercessor*. Both series were subsequently published as pamphlets. This volume combines both booklets since they both deal essentially with the same truth, the authority of the believer.

The Authority of the Believer

There are few subjects relating to the Christian life concerning which there is so little exact knowledge as that of the authority of the believer. This is not because such authority is the property of only a few elect souls. On the contrary, it is the possession of every true child of God. It is one of the "all things" received in Christ. Its reception dates from the soul's contact with Calvary.

Probably because of the extreme importance of a correct understanding of its privileges and responsibilities, and because of the power which they confer on a militant believer, the enemy has specially sought to hold back this knowledge from God's people. He has been successful through the employment of the "blinding" tactics which he has found effective in the case of the "lost" and of those who "believe not" (2 Corinthians 4:3-4). For it is strangely true that, although its principles are set forth in a definite way in the epistle to the Ephesians, there is very little grasp of them by the majority of even spiritual believers.

That there is such authority is recognized, but it is confounded with other aspects of the life of faith, and thereby loses its distinctive value and power. Every doctrine of Scripture, while correlated closely with others of the same class, has features peculiar to itself. Only as these are clearly understood, and held in their right relationship, can there be the fullest benefit from their reception. The constitution and laws of the spiritual world are perfectly orderly and logical, and must be adhered to and carefully obeyed if the desired and promised result is to be gained.

In making this statement it is not intended to suggest that a logical and intelligent mind can of itself grasp spiritual values, or gain possession of spiritual blessings. Were that possible, the deepest phases of the Christian life would be the possession of the most intellectual. Whereas, it is very definitely asserted by the Spirit of God that, in the apprehension of divine truth, "The wisdom of the wise" is destroyed, and "the understanding of the prudent" brought to naught. Thank God, there is an inner spiritual understanding, conferred through the enlightenment of that same Spirit, which enables "the foolish things of the world to confound the wise" (1 Corinthians 1:27)—this principle being established by God "that no flesh should glory in his presence" (1 Corinthians 1:29).

Wrong Conceptions

The authority of the believer is by some confounded with the fullness of the Spirit. It is taught that the coming of the gracious Spirit of God into the soul in His divine fullness gives authority. But the believer's authority exists before he seeks or realizes in any special way the Spirit's presence. It is certainly true that the fullness of the Spirit empowers and enlightens the believer. By this alone he is enabled to exercise authority. But the fullness is not the source of the authority, but something apart from it.

Nor can authority be regarded as some special gift conferred, whereby the recipient is endued with power, by virtue of which he performs mighty acts, such as the casting out of evil spirits. Discernment of spirits and miraculous powers are mentioned among the *charismata* of the Holy Spirit, but they differ from authority.

By others, the authority of the believer is looked upon as nothing more than prevailing prayer. We have heard men on their knees, when under a special urge, giving thanks to God for the gift of prayer conferred at the time. But later there has been no result seen from the agony or enthusiasm of intercession through which they have passed. Personal blessing has resulted from the intense seeking of God's face, but a specific answer to their supplications has not been manifest.

What Authority Is

Let us, first of all, define the difference between "authority" and "power." In the New Testament the translators have not been uniform in the rendering of many words, and these two words have suffered among others. One notable instance is in Luke 10:19 where "power" (KJV) is twice used, although there is a different Greek word in each instance. To have translated the first of these by the English word "authority" would have given a clearer idea of the meaning of the passage. Perhaps our good old English tongue is at times to blame in not providing sufficient synonyms to meet the demands of the original. But a little more uniformity in rendering the same word from the original by the same English equivalent (a thing usually, though not always, possible) would have given greater clearness of understanding, although in places it might not have been so euphonious.

One stands at the crossing of two great thoroughfares. Crowds of people are surging by; multitudes of high-powered vehicles rush along. Suddenly a man in uniform raises a hand. Instantly the tide of traffic ceases. He beckons to the waiting hosts on the cross street, and they flow across in an irresistible wave. What is the explanation? The traffic officer has very little "power." His most strenuous efforts could not avail to hold back one of those swiftly passing cars. But he has something far better. He is invested with the "authority" of the corporation whose servant he is. The moving crowds recognize this authority and obey it.

Authority, then, is delegated power. Its value depends upon the force behind the user. There is a story told of the Right Honorable W.E. Gladstone when he served as Prime Minister of Great Britain. On one occasion he brought in to Queen Victoria an important measure for her signature, in order that it might become law. The queen objected to it, and after some discussion, refused to sign. The Minister of the Crown was unusually urgent: "Your Majesty," he said, respectfully but firmly, "you must sign this bill." She turned on him haughtily: "Sir, I am the Queen of England." Unmoved, the statesman answered quietly, "Your Majesty, I am the *people* of England." After a little thought, she accepted the situation and affixed her signature to the document.

This story may be apocryphal, but it illustrates the question of authority when two opposing powers are in conflict. The believer, who is fully conscious of divine Power behind him, and of his own authority thereby, can face the enemy without fear or hesitation. Those who confront him bear the specific names of power and authority: "We wrestle not against flesh and blood, but against principalities (*archas*, the first or preeminent ones), against powers (*exousias*, the authorities)" (Ephesians 6:12). But, behind the "authority" possessed by the believer, there is a "Power" infinitely greater than that which backs his enemies, and which they are compelled to recognize.

The Source of Authority

In the beginning of this article, we made the statement that the soul's authority dates from its contact with Calvary. Let us now point out the meaning and the depth of this truth. When the Lord Jesus, the Captain (*Archegonn*, Prince-Leader) of our salvation, was raised from the dead, the act of resurrection was accomplished through "the exceeding greatness of his [God's] power [*dunameos*], to usward who believe, according to the working [*energeian*] of the strength [*kratous*] of His might [*ischuos*]." In this working there was such a putting forth of the divine omnipotence that the Holy Spirit, through the apostle, requires four words of special significance to bring out the thought. We shall not enter into the expressive meaning and grouping of these words further than to say that their combination signifies that behind the fact of the resurrection of the Lord Jesus there lay the mightiest working recorded in the Word of God.

Having been thus raised from among the dead, Christ Jesus was exalted by God to His own right hand in the heavenlies. Then was seen the reason of such mighty working. The resurrection had been opposed by the tremendous *"powers of the air"*:—"all principality, and power, and might, and dominion, and every name that is named, not only in this world [*aion*, age] but also in that which is to come" (Ephesians 1:21). The evil forces of the "age to come" had been arrayed against the purpose of God. They had, however, been baffled and overthrown, and the risen Lord had been enthroned "far above" them, ruling with the authority of the Most High.

The Conferring of Authority

In calling attention to the "exceeding greatness of his [God's] power," we passed over without comment four words. These are *"to usward* who believe." All the demonstration of the glory of God, shown in the manifestation of His omnipotence, pointed manward. The cross of Christ, with what it revealed of obedience to God, of atonement for sin, of crushing defeat of the foes of divine authority, shows us a representative Man overcoming for mankind and preparing, through His own incumbency, a throne and a heavenly ministry for those who should overcome through Him.

Observe in this connection the identification of Christ's people with Himself, in this crisis of the resurrection. In the first verse of chapter 2, the words read literally, "And you, *being dead* in trespasses and sins." It will be noticed that we have left out the verb "hath he quickened" which appears in our Bibles. This verb is not in the original; the sentence is incomplete, "being left unfinished," says one expositor, "in the rapidity of dictation." We do not accept this as the explanation of the omission, for we believe that the Holy Spirit so arranged the structure of the whole passage that the fact might be emphasized that Christ and His people were raised together.

Where, then, do we find the verb that controls this passage? It will be seen in verses 19 and 20 of chapter 1: "According to that working of the strength of His might *when* He *raised HIM from the dead* . . ." [then, parentheses should be placed around the words in chapter 1] . . . *and YOU when ye were dead.*" The same verb which expresses the reviving of Christ expresses also the reviving of His people. That is to say the very act of God which raised the Lord from among the dead, raised also His body. Head and body are naturally raised together: Christ, the Head; His body, the Church [*ho ekklesia*, the assembly of believers in Him]. This is a most important statement, and one of which the definite significance cannot be overestimated.

The same thought, in another form, is developed by the apostle in Romans 6, where the death and resurrection of the Lord Jesus are shown to also include His people. The passage in Romans sets forth (1) the death to sin of the believer with the crucified Christ and (2) the consequent annulling of the power of sin over him through the impartation of the life of the resurrected Christ. The believer is thus made a full partaker of Christ's righteousness. But Ephesians lifts (3) the believer with the ascended Christ to the heavenlies where he is made a partaker of Christ's throne. In this enthronement, there is an anticipation of that future union in the government of the nations which he shall share with his Lord, ruling them with a rod of iron and breaking them in pieces like a potter's vessel (Revelation 2:26-27).

The Location of Authority

That there may be no misunderstanding of the Holy Spirit's meaning in this presentation of the truth of the elevation of the Lord's people with their Head, He gives it a second time in Ephesians 2:4-6. They are made to sit with Christ "in the heavenlies." Christ's seat is at the right hand of God. His people, therefore, occupy "with him" the same august position. This honor is not to a chosen few, but is the portion of all those who share the resurrection of the Son of God. It

8

is the birthright of every true believer, of every born-again child of God.

When the Master foregathered with eleven on the Galilean mountain, at some time during the forty days of His manifestation after His passion, He said to them, "All authority is given unto me in heaven and in earth" (Matthew 28:18). His formal assumption of that authority took place when He sat down "on the right hand of the throne of the Majesty in the heavens" (Hebrews 8:1). The right hand of the throne of God is the center of power of the whole universe, and the exercising of the power of the throne was committed unto the ascended Lord. He is still there in full possession of His rights, awaiting the Father's time when His enemies shall be made the footstool of His feet.

The elevation of His people with Him to the heavenlies has no other meaning than that they are made sharers, potentially for the present, of the authority which is His. They are made to sit with Him; that is, they share His throne. To share a throne means without question to partake of the authority which it represents. Indeed, they have been thus elevated in the plan of God, for this very purpose, that they may even now exercise, to the extent of their spiritual apprehension, authority over the powers of the air and over the conditions which those powers have brought about on the earth and are still creating through their ceaseless manipulations of the minds and circumstances of mankind.

The Rebel Holders of This Authority

It is necessary to state here what is commonly understood by those who carefully study the Word, that the kingdoms of this world are under the control and leadership of satanic principalities. The great head of these is, in the Gospel of John, three times acknowledged as "prince of this world" by our Lord Himself. His asserted claim to the suzerainty of the world kingdoms, made in the presence of the Lord Jesus (Luke 4:6), was not denied by Christ. Although a rebel against the Most High and now under judgment of dispossession (John 12:31), he is still at large, and as the masses of mankind are also rebels, he maintains over them an unquestioned, because unsuspected, rule, their eyes being blinded to his dominance (2 Corinthians 4:4).

The whole rebellious system is divided into heavenly and earthly sections (Isaiah 24:21). These are "the host of the high ones that are on high" (the unseen powers of the air) and "the kings of the earth upon the earth" (the rulers of mankind and their subjects). Both, the prophet tells us, will be judged in that day when "the LORD cometh out of his place to punish the inhabitants of the earth for their iniquity" (Isaiah 26:21), and "with his hard and great and strong sword will punish Leviathan the swift serpent [the antichrist], and leviathan the crooked serpent [the false prophet]; and he will slay the monster that is in the sea [the dragon]" (Isaiah 27:1, ASV). Before these acts of judgment occur, the Lord's people will be caught up in the rapture. As Isaiah's eyes were holden to the mystery of the Church, he does not mention it, but he does speak of the hiding of the Jewish remnant from the wrath of the dragon: "Come, my people, enter thou into thy chambers, and shut thy doors about thee: hide thyself . . . for a little moment, until the indignation be overpast" (Isaiah 26:20).

The "host of the high ones on high" is carefully divided in our epistle (Ephesians 6:12). There are first the "principalities and powers." The first-named are mighty princes, whose principalities include large areas of the earth, with authority over the nations included in them. The "powers" are difficult to distinguish from them, although attempts have been made to state the difference; they are inferior in position, probably as ministers associated in government.

Following come "the world rulers of the darkness of this age." This name would suggest a ministry of deception, the keeping in darkness of the minds of men and especially of the leaders of thought.

Finally, there are "the hosts of wicked spirits in the heavenlies"—an innumerable body of demons, to whose close connection with mankind is due the grosser sins and deceptions, the stirring up of the animal passions and the incitement to all manner of sensual and sensuous desires. These are the beings that are present in the spiritist seance, impersonating and deceiving people of strong intelligence, like the well-known leaders connected with the cult today.

These beings are also at hand in religious gatherings and are a source of peculiar danger, especially when the emotions are deeply stirred. Many earnest souls, who have been urged to entire surrender, open their beings with the utmost abandon to whatever spiritual force approaches them, unaware of the peril of so doing. Such yielding often provides an opening for the entrance of demons, who under some pretext gain control of the will. To dislodge them and to once more free the victim is usually a very difficult task.

The "kings of the earth upon the earth" comprise human world rulers and their subjects, all unregenerate men. An earthly ruler individually may be a Christian, but he is, by virtue of his office, a member of the great world system which has not yet come under the dominion of the King of kings. All natural men are members by birth also of this system, and so must be "delivered out of the power (*exousias*, authority) of darkness, and translated into the kingdom of his dear Son" (Colossians 1:13).

The seats of authority of these rebellious spiritual rulers are also in the heavenlies. From there they have dominated the human race since its fall. There they will remain until the divine "purpose of the ages" is complete.

2

The Divine Purpose of the Ages

The "God of the whole earth" does not purpose to tolerate forever this rebellion against His righteousness. "I have sworn by myself, the word is gone out of my mouth in righteousness, and shall not return, That unto me every knee shall bow, every tongue shall swear" (Isaiah 45:23). Ere this can be accomplished, the instigators of human rebellion must be cast down. In this regard the divine method is clear. "The powers of the air" are allowed to retain their seats only while their successors are being prepared. God, having redeemed a people and purified them, has introduced them potentially into the heavenlies. When they have approved themselves, they will in actuality take the seats of the "powers of the air," thereby superseding those who have manifested their unfitness and unworthiness.

This purpose, present and future, is very definitely stated in Ephesians chapter 3:9-11. Here it is revealed as the divine will that "now (*nun*, the present time) unto the principalities and powers in the heavenly places might be made known *through the church* the manifold wisdom of God" (3:10). The Church is to be God's instrument in declaring to these rebellious and now usurping powers the divine purpose, and in administering their principalities after they have been unseated and cast down.

This is further declared to be "according to the eternal purpose of the ages which he purposed in Christ Jesus our Lord" (3:11). That is to say, God, through all the past ages, has had in view this wonderful plan of preparing in Christ Jesus a people, chosen and called and faithful, whom He might place in these heavenly seats to rule through the ages yet to come. It is spoken of, in the verses just preceding, as "the mystery, which for ages hath been hid in God," one phase of this mystery being the wonderful veiling of the deity of the Son of God in our human nature, that we through Him might "become partakers of the divine nature" (2 Peter 1:4).

This exaltation of the saints and its object were revealed to Daniel in the first of his own great world visions. In verse 22 of chapter 7, after the coming of the Ancient of Days, "judgment was given to the *saints of the most High*;[1] and the time came that the saints possessed the kingdoms." A little later (7:27), we read that "the kingdom and the dominion, and the greatness of the kingdom *under the whole heaven*, shall be given to the *people of the saints* of the Most High." This meaning is clear. The saints of the Most High are the overcoming Church, raised to sit in the heavenlies. Below them, and as objects of their care, are the people of Israel, called here "the people of the saints of the most High." Israel will administer the earthly kingdom and will be head of the nations, but overall will rule the exalted Church as the executive of God.

The Extent of This Authority

We shall turn again to chapter 1 of Ephesians and consider in detail the powers and things that have been made subject to our Lord in His exaltation to the Father's right hand. As we meditate on the completeness of His authority, let us remember that He is there as the Representative of redeemed humanity (Hebrews 2:5-9). And may "the eyes of [our] understanding be enlightened" (Ephesians 1:18) by the Holy Spirit so that we may believe, without any doubt or shrinking, that the wisdom and will of the Father have made us sharers of this same authority, and that He verily intends that we should exercise it day by day in growing comprehension and apprehension.

Made to Sit

We notice, first of all, that the Risen Christ has been "made to sit."

The act of sitting indicates that, for the time being, certain aspects of His work are in abeyance. Later, the Lord will again "rise up to the prey." But just now, with "all authority" delivered unto Him, He is awaiting the Father's time, and meanwhile exercising the powers placed in His hands for the working out of the redemption purchased from mankind on Calvary.

Far Above

His session is "all principality, and power, and might, and dominion" (1:21).

The great princes and authorities, of whom we have previously spoken, are subject to Him. So are the lesser ones; He is far above all "might" (*dunameos*, a word usually used in the New Testament of spiritual power). This refers to that working of satanic energy which is becoming increasingly manifest, directed as it is against the bodies and minds of the children of God. The inroads that are being made into Christian communities are appalling, but few in the Church are as yet awake to the fact that fresh powers from the unseen world are flooding in upon us. Nor is the cause of this hard to trace. In parts of the heathen world, where the Word of God energized by the Spirit of God has penetrated, the powers of the air have fallen back. Demon possession ever retires before an aggressive evangelism, and its manifestations become less frequent. But in our so-called Christian lands, the authority of the Word is now called in question by the great leaders of the churches, and there are few theological institutions where it is recognized as the very Word of God. In like manner, the Spirit of God is dishonored, first, by this very denial of the Word which He has inspired, and second, by the disregard paid to His Person and authority. Thus, there is a reversion to heathen conditions spiritually, and as the great agents for the overthrow of demonic powers (the Word of God and the Spirit of God) are discredited, these powers are pressing in again upon our country and people. One single evidence of this fact is the tremendous advance that spiritism is making among all classes: while, as another proof, the very doctrines of the Church, depleted of their vital spiritual force as they are becoming, are showing undoubted marks of those "teachings of demons" of which the great apostle bade his hearers beware.

Christ sits also far above all "dominion" (*kuriotetos*, lordship). This term is closely allied with the preceding, much as "principalities and powers" are grouped together, the second term in each case signifying similar action on a somewhat lower plane. In Colossians 1:16, we find "dominion" connected with "thrones," which throws light upon the relative term "might." In the passage in Ephesians and in that quoted from Colossians, both terms refer directly to spiritual powers, whereas in Second Peter 2:10 and Jude 8, the only two other occasions of the use of the word in the New Testament, the primary reference is to earthly dignities.

In This Age

He sits far above "every name that is named, not only in this world" (*aion*, age) (1:21); the great names of this age are below our Lord. The writer of Hebrews took pains to point out to Israel that even Moses was inferior to Messiah (Christ), as a servant is less than his Master. But what an effort religious leaders are mak-

17

ing today to show that Jesus was only a man, and as such to be ranked with the best men. Over the door of one of the great church buildings of New York, appear figures of some world famous men—such as Emerson, Einstein, Confucius, Buddha, etc., and with them the figure of Christ as one among many! Not so speaks the Spirit of Truth; in His setting forth of the majesty of the Divine Son of God, there are none that can be compared; He is "far above" all. In this continued attempt to exalt humanity, there is to be recognized the working of him who deceived our first parents with the falsehood, "Ye shall be as gods."

The Age to Come

"But also in that which is to come" (1:21). The coming age also yields no name that ranks with that of our Lord. In that age, moreover, the now-dominant spirit-forces shall be bound. Their successors, the glorified Church, shall recognize the preeminence of their exalted King. United with Him as Head and Body, they will have become manifestly His "fullness." He fills "all in all," but has chosen to do so through His Body. Thus, in the age to come, the members of Christ shall have an active ministry for God throughout the limitless extent of His universe.

Under His Feet

"Hath put all things under his feet" (1:22). The feet are members of the Body. How wonderful to think that the least and lowest members of the Body of the Lord, those who in a sense are the very soles of the feet, are far above all the mighty forces we have been considering. Yet so it is. What need for the Church to awake to an appreciation of her mighty place of privilege. Exalted to rule over the spiritual powers of the air, how often she fails in her ministry of authority or grovels before them in fear.

Head over All

"Head over all things to the church" (1:22). We have little grasped the force of this marvelous truth. We think of it as if it indicated that Christ was simply in all things and circumstances and places the Church's Head. Let us reverse the words to bring out more clearly their deep significance: "Head to the church over all things." His being Head over all things is for the Church's sake, that the Church, His Body, may be head over all things through Him. We need to sit reverently and long before these mighty truths, that their tremendous meaning may grasp our hearts. In this attitude, the Spirit of Truth can lift us into their comprehension, which the human mind alone will always fail to compass.

The Operation of God

The argument which we have been following has been thus far centered in the Epistle to the Ephesians. We pass, for a few minutes, to the Epistle to the Colossians, that we may view from a different standpoint how completely this whole matter of the authority of the believer is based on the working of the Father, and how the efficacy of that working depends on the correlated truth of the subjection of Christ to Him. Though coequal with the Father, the Eternal Son accepted a subordinate place, and undertook the task of reconciling, through the blood of His cross, all things unto God (1:20). Having for this purpose yielded Himself under the power of death, He was quickened by "the operation of God" the Father (2:12).

Let us read carefully 2:12-15, noting that the working here indicated is all on the part of God the Father. It is He who (2:13) quickened the saints together with Christ and forgave their trespasses. It is He who (2:14) blotted out the adverse decrees of the law, which stood in the way of His people and nailed the canceled handwriting to the cross of His Son. It is He who (2:15) spoiled (*apekdusamenos*, completely stripped) the mighty principalities and powers that had opposed the resurrection of the Lord and led them captive in triumphal procession in Christ.

A frequent misunderstanding of this passage is that the Lord Jesus "stripped off" from Himself the clustering powers of darkness, overthrowing and putting them to an open shame. But a correct rendering shows clearly that the Agent is God the Father. Of what does He "strip" the powers of the air? Of the authority that had been theirs. Death is the penalty of sin; and when Christ, bearing the burden of the world's guilt, went down to death, they sought to exercise their ancient prerogative and hold Him under its power. But in the wisdom of the Father, the yielding of the Righteous One to death discharged the long-established bond of the Law. Exultantly, the Father nailed the canceled bond to the cross of His Son; then, "stripping" of their authority the discomfited principalities and powers, He handed this authority to His Son. The "show" (triumphal procession), which the apostle figuratively uses, corresponds to the elevation of the Son above His enemies, mentioned in Ephesians.

Thus, in Colossians there is stressed the Father's working in the active thwarting and overthrowing of the hostile powers and their subjugation to His Son, while in Ephesians the Son is seen seated above these in all the authority of the Father's throne. The authority of the believer is not taught so fully in Colossians, although the statement is made that in Him His people are "complete" (literally, made full). That is to say, through union with Him, they partake of the fullness of the Godhead, which is practically another form of being "blessed with all spiritual blessings."

The Failure of the Church

We saw in a previous section the Lord as Head over all. His position and power are supreme. Why, then, is there not more manifest progress? Because a head is wholly dependent upon its body for the carrying out of its plan. All the members of its body must be subservient, that through their coordinated ministry may be accomplished what is purposed. The Lord Jesus, "Head over all things to the church, which is *His* body" (Ephesians 1:22-23), is hindered in His mighty plans and working, because His Body has failed to appreciate the deep meaning of His exaltation and to respond to the gracious impulses which He is constantly sending for its quickening.

The Word of God

It is a most vital truth of the divine working that the Word of God is the pattern by which the ministry of the Church is framed. The glory of the Body of Christ is the fact that its members are living members, each with a personal will. The Holy Spirit comes into these individual members in order to bring them into unity with the will and purposes of the Head. But this is not done through inward impulse alone. Inward impulse inaugurates obedience toward the Head, but the renewed mind cannot be fully instructed save through the Word. Consequently, it is only as the Word is carefully meditated upon, understood and obeyed that the Head has freedom of action through its members. How little the average member feeds with careful mastication upon the Word, most of us know from our own experience.

The Spirit of God

The importance of this can be seen by comparing Ephesians 5:18ff, with Colossians 3:16ff. In the first passage, the stirring of the inward emotions of the heart, with the consequent subjection of believers one to another, in their various relations, is indicated as the working of the Spirit of God in His fullness, but in the second passage, exactly the same results are pointed out to be the result of the rich indwelling of the Word of Christ. The Word of Christ is the setting forth of

His will in a form that is understandable by the renewed mind. But the renewed mind, while understanding the Word, lacks power to perform it. The fullness of the Spirit is the incoming of the Spirit of God to empower the human spirit for the carrying into effect of the accepted will of the Head.

Thus, unless the Word richly indwells for the instruction of the mind, the Spirit of God, although present in His fullness, has nothing to work upon. The impulses of the Head cannot be translated by Him into appropriate action through the Body, but are often like the immature motions of a child. The Head is thereby hindered because the Body has not grown up into the stature of a perfect man. In divine patience the Head waits. Brethren, we are to blame greatly, not only for our own weakness, but also for "the hands that hang down and the palsied knees." God help us to realize this and to fulfill our ministry through the Word both to others and to the Lord.

Note

1 The word translated "most high" has the significance of "elevated," and is rendered "high places" in the margin of one edition. This would correspond very closely with the "heavenlies" of our epistle.

3

The Qualifications for Authority

It has been pointed out more than once in this study that the authority of which we are speaking is the portion of every believer. It is not a special gift imparted in answer to prayer but the inherent right of the child of God because of his elevation with Christ to the right hand of the Father. He has become, through the rich mercy of God, an occupant of the throne of the Lord, with all that it implies of privilege and responsibility.

This elevation took place potentially at the resurrection of the Lord because of the believer's inclusion in Him. The elevation is wholly of the wisdom and grace of the Father. We do not "climb the heavenly steeps" by any act of faith or devotion on our part. It is ours simply to recognize the fact of this position and to take our place in humble acceptance, giving all the glory and honor to God.

Let us recall four words to which mention has been previously made. They are *"to usward* who believe" (Ephesians 1:19). In the former reference we emphasized the first two, pointing out that all the demonstration of the omnipotence of God to Christ pointed manward. We shall now lay stress upon the latter two: "to usward *who believe.*" It is not enough that the divine Fullness outpours unstinted supplies; there must be a receptive heart and attitude on our part. A bottle may be submerged in the waters of a fountain. But if the cork is not removed, the holder may wait indefinitely and at last carry it away empty. In accord with this simile, multitudes of truly spiritual believers are, as it were, immersed in the omnipotence of God; it presses them on every side. There is a longing for its experience and a belief that it should be theirs and a readiness to receive, these things being the witness of their spirits to the truth which the Holy Ghost has unfolded in the Word. Yet, because their minds have been "holden" as they have read the Word, the simplicity and the glory of this truth have not dawned upon them. Do we not need, indeed, continually to pray with deep heart-humility that "the eyes of [our] mind may be enlightened" (Ephesians 1:18)?

Belief

"To usward *who believe*" (1:19). Few comprehend the primary thought of "belief." It has a twofold meaning, fraught with deep significance. In it are combined two old Anglo-Saxon words: "be," to live or exist; and "lifan," which conveys the thought of accordance. Thus to believe means literally "to live in accordance with" anything. We are accustomed to consider "belief" as simply mental acquiescence with some particular truth. But its root leads us to action; that which the mind accepts, the will must obey. We do not truly believe, therefore, unless our conviction is manifested in our life. Thus understood, "belief" stands on a par with its great synonym "faith," which in its deeper sense means not only to have trust in a person but to manifest that trust by practical committal.

Do we believe that God "hath quickened us together with Christ and hath raised us up together, and made us sit together in heavenly places in Christ Jesus" (Ephesians 2:5-6)? If we do, our reaction to it will be a fervent, "Lord, I accept Thy gracious word. I believe that Thou hast thus wrought for me. In humble faith I do now take my seat in the heavenly places in Christ Jesus at Thy right hand. Teach me how to fulfill this sacred ministry, how to exercise the authority which Thou hast entrusted to me. Train me day by day that I may attain to the full stature of the perfect man in Christ, so that in me Thy purpose of the ages may be fulfilled. Amen."

If we are walking in the Spirit, our normal life is in the heavenlies. To secure the consciousness of this, there must be the daily acceptance of the fact. Let us, morning by morning, as one of our first acts of worship, take our seat with Christ (as suggested in the previous paragraph) and return thanks to God for all that it implies. Let us often remind ourselves that we are

27

seated far above all the powers of the air, and that they are in subjection to us. As our faith learns to use the Name and the Authority of Jesus, we shall find the spiritual forces yielding obedience in ways that will surprise us. As we continue to abide closely in Him, our prayers for the advancement of the kingdom will become less and less the uttering of petitions and will increasingly manifest the exercise of a spiritual authority that recognizes no national boundaries, but fearlessly binds the forces of darkness in any part of the world.

Humility

While belief thus introduces us to our place of throne power, only humility will ensure our retaining it. As we compare the abounding grace of God and our own utter unworthiness, the question arises: Should we need such a warning? Praise God, it becomes less necessary as the soul grows in grace and the likeness of the Son increases in us. But we know little of the plague of our own hearts if we think the danger is ever over. The forces against whom we contend, the principalities and powers, the world rulers of this darkness, the hosts of wicked spirits in the heavenlies, know us far better than we know ourselves. As we attack them, and authority is nought but a long-drawn-out warfare against them, their return stroke is often swift and crushing. With a strategy gained in long experience in spiritual battles, they know that the offensive is their best mode of defense. One of their tested weapons is spiritual pride, and too often it proves effective.

Victory over the powers of the air, from their dread prince downward, is a demonstrated possibility. But its attainment is alone through the employment of divine aid. Now, since Eden, man has forgotten that God is essential; through the intervening ages he has constantly sought to show himself self-sufficient. Christ was the first of all our race that ever cast Himself fully upon God. "He trusted in God; let him deliver him" (Matthew 27:43) was the sneer of the enemy of Calvary. But at Calvary, the One who had thus fully trusted could not be delivered. He must go down to death, for the sin question of the world was involved and the shedding of His precious blood was necessary for atonement. So "He was crucified through weakness" (2 Corinthians 13:4). When this was accomplished, nothing more stood in the way. God raised Him from the dead, stripped His foes of their authority and set Him on high over them.

With believers, the consuming desire to be independent is something which even the regenerated heart does not fully overcome. Often, just after some signal victory has been gained, there comes the subtle whisper of the enemy, and the overcomer is swiftly shorn of strength through feeling that he is strong.

Boldness

With profound humility, however, there may go the greatest boldness in the Name. True boldness is faith in full manifestation. When God has spoken, to hold back is not humility but unbelief. In the exercise of authority, there is needed a divine courage that fears nothing but God and reaches out strong hands to bind and to restrain all that is contrary to Him. But with this courage, there must be a continual and close abiding in God, a spirit that is alert to every urge and check from Him and a mind that is steeped in the Word of God.

Fear

The heavenlies, while the place of "every spiritual blessing" (Ephesians 1:3), are also the place of most intense conflict. Let the believer, whose eyes have been opened to the comprehension of his throne rights in Christ, definitely accept his seat and begin to exercise the spiritual authority which it confers upon him. He quickly realizes that he is a marked man. Whereas in his previous ministry he may have firmly believed in the presence and working of the powers of darkness and often earnestly prayed against them, there comes now a new consciousness of their existence and imminence. Bitterly they resent and resist his entrance into their domain and his interference with their workings. Implacable and malignant, they concentrate their hatred against him in an intense warfare in which there is no discharge. If attacks against his spirit are successfully resisted, assaults may come in mind, body, family or circumstances.

The place of special privilege thus becomes a place of special danger. That there is no truth that encounters such opposition in its presentation is the testimony of those who have brought it forward by voice or pen. We have known of workers who have taught these truths with acceptance, who have been quite overthrown in spirit or in body, and their ministry rendered useless. Yet since God Himself, with an eternal purpose in view, has introduced His people into this sphere, we cannot doubt that full provision has been made for their safety.

The Panoply of God

The only place of safety is the occupation of the seat itself. It is "far above" the enemy. If the believer abides steadfastly by faith in this location, he cannot be touched. Consequently the enemy puts forth all his "wiles" to draw him down in spirit, for once out of his seat, his authority is gone, and he is no longer dangerous, and further, he is open to attack.

At this point is seen the meaning of the message of Ephesians chapter 6. To maintain his place against the wiles of the devil, the believer must be constantly arrayed in full armor. The different parts of this armor symbolize certain spiritual attitudes which he must maintain. It is most important to understand that the armor itself, when worn, constitutes the protection of the believer and not his activity against the foe. Fully harnessed, he is fully kept and is unhampered in his ministry of authority. All that he need be concerned about is, like a good soldier, to keep his armor bright and well secured about him.

Let us note briefly the meaning of the various parts of the panoply: No item can be omitted. There is (1) "The girdle of truth" (6:14), the clear understanding of God's Word, which, like a soldier's belt holds the rest of the armor in place. (2) "The breastplate of right-eousness" (6:14, not, as often stated, the righteousness of Christ, but rather the active obedience to the Word which he has received. (3) The "feet shod with the preparation of the gospel of peace" (6:15), a faithful ministry in the heralding of the Word. (4) "The shield of faith" (6:16) (*thureos*, the large door-shaped shield covering the whole body), which indicates his complete refuge under the blood of Calvary, where no power of the enemy can penetrate. (5) "The helmet of salvation" (6:17) (called elsewhere "the hope of salvation," 1 Thessalonians 5:8). It is a remarkable fact that the hope of salvation, the coming of the Lord Jesus, is the only helmet that seems able to protect the head in these days of apostasy from the truth. (6) "The sword of the Spirit" (6:17), which shows the Word of God used in an active sense, even as the "girdle" shows it in a defensive one. (7) "All-prayer" (6:18), the training of the faculties Godward by constant approach to God.

The emphasis in chapter 6 is laid on victory. Note the following paraphrase which brings out the full force of verse 13: "Wherefore take up with you to the battle the whole armor of God, that you may be able to successfully withstand in the evil day, and having overthrown all foes, to remain unshaken." There is no suggestion of defeat. Secure within his armor, the believer may disregard the enemy and give his entire attention to the exercise of the ministry to which he has been called.

4

The Practical Exercise of Authority

The believer has now accepted the place of exaltation with his Lord. There has opened for him a life of holiness in the presence of God, and of watchfulness in the presence of the enemy in a deeper sense than he has known before. His first lesson will be personal. He must learn the significance of the term "Satan" (the adversary) and come to understand why one of his titles is "accuser of the brethren" (Revelation 12:10). Just as Joshua (Zechariah 3:1), when he came to stand before the Angel of Jehovah, found "Satan standing at his right hand to be his adversary" (ASV), so will the spiritually energetic child of God. He will encounter a constant stream of accusations in his own heart. These will trouble him until he discovers that the purpose of the enemy is to turn him in upon himself and, through the creating of a consciousness of personal unworthiness, draw him down from the place of perfect faith. He learns to "[overcome] him by the blood of the Lamb" (Revelation 12:11). That is to say, he presents the blood as his only answer to these accusations.

But he speedily learns a further use for this divine provision. The blood represents not only the cleansing from the guilt and power of sin, but it is also the witness of that overwhelming victory gained at Calvary by virtue of which the Lord is now seated on high. Once this is grasped, the believer sees that he does not have to fight against the foe but simply to hold over him an already accomplished triumph, the authority of which he shares in the full. Not all at once the full vision comes, but, as he holds his place and exercises his ministry, there will be a gradual perfecting in the heavenly warfare. It will be in his province, concerning the hosts of darkness, "to bind their kings with chains, and their nobles with fetters of iron," and, in that approaching day of full exaltation in the presence of the King, "to execute upon them the judgment written." Oh, that all God's people might come to an understanding of their high calling, for it is expressly stated: "This honor have all his saints" (Psalm 149:8-9).

The Limitation of Authority

Let it ever be held in mind that the authority committed to the believer is over the powers of the air and never over his fellowmen or their wills. He is called to bind the unseen forces but to deliver his brethren. Satan's constant aim is the subjugation of the human will to himself; God's purpose is the full liberation of the will that the freed spirit, through glad acquiescence in the divine will, may glorify his Creator. Human control of the will of another, as manifested in hypnotism, etc., is obtained through the use of occult powers latent in the soul and is as unlawful for the Christian as wizardry and necromancy, which are directly forbidden in the Word of God. Following are a few simple examples of authority in exercise.

Release from Oppression of Body

Just a year prior to this writing, contact was made in a country district with an earnest young pastor and his equally efficient wife—equally efficient in spirit, at least, but in body sorely hindered. For long she had suffered from what had been diagnosed as serious heart trouble for which medical treatment was being taken. One symptom was the frequent recurrence of severe pains, causing fainting spells. The husband stated that he had several times, on coming into the house, found her lying unconscious on the floor.

The wife mentioned that her father was a spiritist and that she had been expert in former days with the planchette. The question was asked, "Is it not probable, sister, that your present physical trouble and your difficulty in receiving healing is due to the past?" "No," was the serious reply, "for I was never a medium in the ordinary sense. I simply used the planchette," and many interesting and remarkable incidents of its use were narrated. "Nevertheless," the point was pressed, "in using the planchette, your body had to be surrendered to the evil spirit. There is little question in my mind that the difficulty lies there.

Your connection with these powers should be acknowledged and confessed. Then a definite stand in the authority of the Lord should be taken, absolutely refusing the further working of evil spirits in your body, which has been purchased by the precious blood."

About three weeks after, a letter was received from the sister in question. After the visitor's departure, the light had come; confession had been made and she and her husband had unitedly refused the further oppression of the enemy. She has never had another attack of heart trouble and has been blessed in her service greatly.

Release from Oppression of Mind

Some months ago, after a service in one of our cities, two women came asking an interview. The appearance of one gave an immediate understanding of the situation which was confirmed by conversation. There had been earnest seeking of deep spiritual experience which was followed by a sudden attack of intense despondency. The attacks persisted until, after three years, the mind was in complete bondage. All joy had fled and only a feeble hold of salvation was retained. Suggestions of suicide were frequent, pressing with an urgency that was hard to resist.

The following line of approach was taken, after definitely asserting in prayer the power of the ascended Lord, and the believer's throne union with Him. "Sister, this trouble is clearly the oppression of evil spirits, which have obtained a hold over you in some manner. These thoughts of self-destruction are directly prompted by him who is a deceiver and a murderer. You are a Christian and united with Christ. This afternoon may be for you, if you will, the last occasion of manifestation of satanic power." In a simple manner, her place of victory and authority in Christ was shown from the Word. She was urged to take it audibly before those who were witnesses (her sister, a friend and the speaker). After full assertions of her faith and her acceptance of what Christ had gained and the Father had bestowed, the party kneeled in victorious prayer. As the group arose, one of the friends remarked; "She looks different already." There was a life and animation, most noticeable after the deadness of her previous expression.

A few weeks ago, a letter came: "I feel as if I were saved all over again." Joy and peace had returned; the Holy Spirit had come, and soul-saving work had been granted to her.

Authority over Excessive Anger

"Be ye angry, and sin not: let not the sun go down upon your wrath" (Ephesians 4:26), the apostle charges the readers of the epistle we have been studying; "neither give place to the devil." There is an intimate connection between sinful anger and the prince of evil, and sustained wrath will surely open the door to his entrance. In a certain city two Christian workers, husband and wife, had fallen into the enemy's snare of wrath. One day their quarreling had reached a shameful height and was attracting attention, as it had done before. The writer and his wife were within hearing and at prayer. Quietly and definitely they took authority over the spirits of evil who were behind the ostensible cause and commanded their withdrawal. Almost immediately the quarreling stopped. As the authority was day by day and renewed, the spirits were kept in check. Eventually, however, the two separated, for they did not seek victory for themselves.

One of the Filipino workers, when a student in the Bible school, had a very quick and ungovernable temper. This having been stirred up by a trivial matter, he utterly lost control of himself and speedily became almost insane with rage. The principal and writer stepped into the next apartment and, kneeling down, took the authority of the Lord over the spirits that were working upon him. In a few minutes he was quiet, and it was possible to deal with him.

Similar cases occurred in the girls' school. On one occasion, after a fight among them, the ringleader was isolated in the office where she continued shrieking wildly. The writer stepped into the office, sat down and quietly and inaudibly exercised the authority of the Lord, commanding the evil spirits to leave the place. The girl instantly ceased, so suddenly that the lady principal asked what had been done to her.

Authority over Fear

In traveling among the islands off the coast of Mindanao in a native boat, a considerable swell was encountered. The son of the writer began to show fear which became almost uncontrollable. This was most unusual as he was normally fond of the water and was an excellent sailor, having frequently traveled up and down the entire China coast where storms are severe. He begged to be taken ashore, and as the whole affair seemed to be directed against the progress of the evangelistic trip, the writer quietly took the authority of Christ over the spirits of fear and rebuked them, though saying nothing openly. In a very few minutes the lad seemed to change completely, and for the remainder of the journey lasting several days, there was no further difficulty. The second night after, while in the center of a wide bay and about twelve miles from shore, a heavy squall was encountered, and an outrigger broke. The danger was imminent, but, though the lad was fully aware of it, and though the waves were washing quite over the boat, he manifested not the slightest shrinking. Other instances of fear involving older and experienced missionaries are personally known.

Demon Obsession

Coming down the West River, in the south of China, in 1926, there was a man on board being taken to Hong Kong for mental treatment. He was a foreigner and a member of the customs staff in Wuchow. Early in the morning he leaped overboard but was rescued and placed in a cabin on board. A little later he cut his throat from ear to ear. The boat dropped anchor, and native doctors came and sewed and dressed his wounds. After they had left him, the writer was asked to talk with him. He was lying on the cabin bunk with his hands secured by a rope.

As soon as the cabin was entered, and before any question was asked, he said, "They told me to do it."

"Who told you?"

"The voices; they are talking to me all the time. They told me to throw myself overboard; and when I was taken from the water, they said there was no hope for me, as I had tried to take my life, and said I must cut my throat." Then, growing excited, he cried, "They are talking to me now; they say I must send you away. Go! Go!"

He was quite beside himself. The answer was made: "These are demon voices that speak with you. I am not afraid of them. I have come in here to help you."

After prayer, he quieted, and no recurrence of the trouble occurred up to the time he was taken from the boat to the hospital at Hong Kong. He was not delivered, but the trouble was under control while the worker was near. Here it may be said that demons recognize at once anyone who can exercise the authority of the Lord, and they are afraid of him. But full deliverance in such a case as this cannot take place without the consent of the one attacked. Other examples could be given.

Authority over Opposers of the Truth

Previous illustrations are from the personal experiences of the writer. The following is by a lady now deceased. In a town in the north of England, great opposition was being manifested to some religious meetings by a group of the rougher sort, stirred by certain communistic leaders. After a short time, the pastor called some of his people together and asked them to stand with him against the power of the enemy. About a hundred gathered, and after prayer, they definitely repeated with him, "In the name of the Lord Jesus Christ and by His authority we bind the strong man from stirring up these people and from attacking God's work." A hymn of praise was sung, and members dispersed. The very next day trouble rose among the leaders of the opposition, some of them left town and no further hindrance to work was encountered.

Inferences

Such instances as the foregoing might be multiplied, but these have been selected as illustrating different phases of the question. They are sufficient to show that there are many situations where the direct working of spirits of evil may be inferred. In all such situations, the authority of the Lord is available for the instructed believer. And where in faith the obedient saint claims his throne rights in Christ and boldly exerts his authority, the powers of the air will recognize and obey. There may be unwillingness and delay on their part, and time may be required. But once the word of authority is spoken, it is not necessary to repeat it. The believer must "stand" (6:13) and strengthen himself in God as he waits. He will learn with joy, as did the disciples of old, that "even the demons are subject unto us through thy name" (Luke 10:17, ASV).

Apply now these lessons to the great problems of the extension of the kingdom that face us. *Here is the shortage of funds.* We speak of the financial distress, but is any work of the devil today distressed for funds? A walk on the streets of New York after working hours will speedily give the answer. Satan is choking the channels of Christian benevolence in many and shrewd ways, but he leaves free those which minister to pleasure and sensuality. The writer knows intimately of several cases in widely separated parts of the land where funds are tied up which, if released, would be instrumental in the advancement of the gospel.

Here are closed lands. Human governmental authority seems responsible for these. But in the background, there stand the shadowy forms of the great princes (Daniel 10) whose dicta rule the minds and wills of the men whom we see. Afghanistan, Arabia, Tibet and lesser areas are thus garrisoned against the entry of the truth. They will thus remain until there rises in the Church believing groups who shall "agree" that this state of affairs shall no longer continue. And as such bands, with one accord, exercise a spiritual will of freedom for these lands, saying in the name of the Lord, "This shall not be!" the unseen dominant forces shall be dominant no longer but shall yield ground, and the barriers shall fall.

Here are hindrances to advance in the field work. Mohammedanism meets us with bigotry and jealousy; paganism with fear and hatred; ignorance binds the heathen mind in darkness that seems impenetrable. Fierce attacks, such as occurred near the time of this writing in French West Africa, fall upon the workers, and some are cut off. Dissensions rise in the ranks of brethren, and the Spirit of peace withdraws. Behind every such situation the presence of the same malign powers can be assumed. The solution is in their displacement—we alone are to blame that they continue in power.

The same principle is often applicable in personal evangelism. A soul under conviction has great difficulty in grasping the truth or in yielding to it. His mind is blinded and bound. A quiet attitude of victory over the opposing spirits has often brought swift release. A Filipino student was suspected of lying but was resolutely standing by his falsehood. Quietly the position was taken, "In the name of the Lord, I rebuke these lying spirits." Suddenly the student broke down, confessed and wept his way through to victory.

Will it not be worthwhile for the believer to meet in the coming age men and women who have been delivered "out of the snare of the devil" and loosed from varying forms of bondage, because he has steadfastly stood for their deliverance for long periods against the fierce and incessant assaults of these deadly foes?

The Final Outcome of Authority

The question is often asked: Why does God permit this or that condition? Does not the answer lie here? God has planned that man shall, through the outworking of redemption, regain the place of authority in creation that he has lost. To this end, Christ, having conquered for man, sits as his Representative in the seat destined for him when redemption is fully manifested. In the interim, the wonderful provision exists that man shall be reckoned in Christ and shall, to the limit of his spiritual understanding and obedience, be endowed with the authority of His name.

Accordingly, God throws upon man the responsibility for the continuance of the conditions which we question. We feel they ought not to be. We realize that they are the working of the enemy. We cry to God to rebuke the enemy and to alter things. Through the teaching of the Word, He replies, "My children, rebuke the enemy yourselves. The authority over him is yours. Its responsibility I have committed to you. I desire you to learn in these things to prevail. I have purposed a high and holy ministry for you in the coming age. This is for you the time of testing and preparation. Be strong and of a good courage, and none shall be able to stand before you all the days of your life."

Slowly, believers are awaking to their high place of privilege in Christ and are assuming the responsibilities which it involves. The body of the man-child, who is to rule all nations with a rod of iron, is nearing completion. Born of the Church, but not itself the Church, the body consists of many members with widely differing offices. These members are out of every age and people. On its ascension to the throne of God, which now potentially it shares, the rebellious powers of the air which have so long resisted divine authority shall be fully and forever dispossessed of their seats to make room for the new incumbents.

Before that event, it is recorded that "the powers of the heavens shall be shaken." The initial tremors of that shaking are now taking place. Every fully yielded heart that crowns Jesus King increases the consternation of the panic-stricken hosts. Conscious of their impending overthrow, they are seeking by fierce attacks on every front to hold back the final issue. Now is no time for the Church of Christ to hold back. Let us meet attack by counterattack. Faith is needed, courage, determination, sacrifice. We have these—and more, we have Calvary, with all that it means. Men and women are needed who will meet God in all that He offers, who will take up the cause of the closed lands and reply to the challenge of the great heathen religions by an aggressive warfare in the heavenlies.

"Who is on the Lord's side? Who will face the foe?"

5

The Authority of the Intercessor

So unreasonable to the natural mind seems the proposition of Jehovah to His people (Isaiah 45:11) that they should "command" Him concerning the work of His hands, that various alternative readings of the passage have been made with the intent of toning down the apparent extravagance of the divine offer. Men are slow to believe that the Almighty really means exactly what He says. They think it an incredible thing that He should share with human hands the throttle of infinite power. Nor have they the spiritual understanding to comprehend the purpose of the Father to bring those who have been redeemed with the precious blood of His dear Son into living and practical cooperation with that Son in the administration of His kingdom.

The people of Christ are revealed in the New Testament (Ephesians 1:23) as "the fullness of him that filleth all in all." They bear a vital relationship to Him as members of His body, through whom His glorious purposes are to be wrought out in eternity. Consequently it is not a strange thing that, in this present preparatory age, He should make large revelations and offers of His grace in order that He may test the faith and develop the spiritual powers of those who will be sharers of the authority and ministry of His throne through the coming ages. We need have no fear in accepting the fullest implications of the words above referred to, in spite of the critical attitude of even some devout scholars.

The principle involved is set forth in other places of the Word of God, in different phraseology it may be but with equal cogency and clarity. Our duty is to draw near with the boldness of faith and in the attitude and readiness of full obedience. Faith will prove a key to unlock every mystery of the truth; obedience will secure our entrance through the door thus opened. In a new and deeper sense we shall discover ourselves to be sons abiding ever in the great house of the Father, partaking of all its relationships and responsibilities. Its many ministries will become vivid as we move about in them, speaking words of authority and seeing the behests of the Spirit of God which are uttered through us carried out to their fulfillment.

The Counsels of the Heart

In Psalm 20 the coming Messiah is set before us in His human aspect. It is for Him a time of trouble, but the name of the God of Jacob has set Him on high, and divine grace sends forth His help from the sanctuary. His offerings are remembered and accepted before the Most High. Then follows a prophetic petition: "Grant thee according to thine own heart, and fulfill all thy counsel" (20:4). The desires and purposes of this Chosen Servant of God are promised full accomplishment. All of His heart plans are acceptable to Jehovah; they are in full accord with the divine ideals; therefore, a second assurance is given: "The Lord fulfill all thy petitions" (20:5).

The One who is thus addressed is the Son of man, the great Representative of our humanity. Through Him the Spirit of God had unhindered liberty in carrying out the divine counsel during all His earthly career. His human will was in constant and perfect alignment with that of the Father in heaven. No shadow ever rose between Him and God save that thick cloud of our sins which enveloped Him on Calvary. At each step of His daily walk He could say, "I do always the things that please Him." Because this was true, there was no bar to the granting of the desires of His heart or to the fulfillment of His inward counsels.

The deep reality of the union between Christ and His people is but little comprehended by the great majority of believers. It is compared by the Holy Spirit to the relationship of a head to the members of the body over which it is set. Where perfect health prevails, the members are responsive to the slightest impulses of the head. But if disease prevails in any part of the body, there is a lack of full coordination, some member or members being tardy in obedience, or inaccurate in carrying out their rightful functions, or it may be unable to obey at all. The body of Christ differs from the human body in that each member possesses an individual volition which must be surrendered voluntarily to the will of the Head. Much schism, alas, exists also in the body as a whole, and much self-will in the individual member. These things hinder healthy growth and the free outworking of the purposes of Christ. Yet, where any member dwells fully in his place, "holding the Head" (Colossians 2:19), there is not only full cooperation but also true identity of desire with the Lord, and the Master's promise finds occasion of fulfillment: "If ye abide in me, and my words abide in you, ye shall ask what ye will, and it shall be done unto you" (John 15:7).

Note carefully the significance of the statement, "*Ye shall ask what YE will.*" How many believers content themselves with a submissive uttering of the words, "Thy will be done," in all matters which they bring before the Lord. Their spirits assume a passive attitude that accepts anything that comes to them as the will of the Father. This is not scriptural, and it is very far from the desire of God for His children. The Holy Spirit teaches a hearty cooperation rather than mere resignation; an active entering into God's plan instead of a vague yielding to circumstances; a definite claiming and appropriation of the promises which are set before us in the Word, as being the expression of the Father's will for His children. We are to positively will the will of God, to seek it out as He has revealed it and to maintain our place of quiet assurance before Him until it has been fully accomplished.

Dr. E.E. Helms once told how he had promised a bicycle to his son. They went out together to inspect the various models and to make the purchase. The boy led the way to a particular store and indicated a machine which he said was the one he wanted. His father suggested it might be better to look at some others before finally deciding. But the lad was quite sure as to his own mind. "Father," he said, "I've been scouting round already and sized them up, and this is the one I want. I'm going to stay here until I get it." He was successful; and his father in telling the story remarked that if we would take that attitude in our praying there would be fewer unanswered prayers.

This attitude will ensure the carrying out of the promise to the Head: "Jehovah . . . grant thee according to thy heart's desire, and fulfill all thy counsel." The member of the Body has come into complete intimacy with the Head; he discerns the purposes of his Lord; through his purposeful petitions, Christ's own heart's desires are fulfilled. Of not a few of the saints this characteristic has been true in a marked degree. It is not the fault of the Head that it cannot be said of all.

The Sharing Authority

Matthew, in the closing chapter of his Gospel, shows us the King on the mountain in Galilee which He had appointed as the rendezvous for His disciples. He is speaking to the group of followers who surround

Him: "All power is given unto me in heaven and in earth" (Matthew 28:18). It may seem a strange statement to many Christians, but it is nevertheless a profound spiritual truth that the authority of the risen Head at the right hand of the throne of the Majesty in the heavens is planned to reach its full development and manifestation through His Body. The Son of God became incarnate not merely that He might save men from their sins, but also that He might bring man to that place of dominion over the works of God which was planned in the counsels of eternity (Psalm 8:6). Today, the inspired writer tells us (Hebrews 2:9), "we see Jesus" holding in trust for redeemed mankind all that the race has lost through sin. Our Lord has Himself taken the Headship and is forming for Himself a Body through which He will fulfill the original divine purpose.

Much of the weakness of the Church is due to its failure to understand and appropriate this all-important truth. It is ours, as individual members of the body, to seek that the authority of Christ shall come with full acceptance into our spirits. It is not enough to know and acknowledge that He is our fullness; there must be, as well, the apprehension of the complementary truth that we are also His fullness (see Ephesians 1:23). What an amazing honor and dignity is thus purposed for us: "heirs of God, and joint-heirs with Christ" (Romans 8:17). For the coming of age of the body and its entrance upon the inheritance, all the rest of God's creation is waiting with earnest expectation.

The Removal of Mountains

Serious obstacles often confront the servant of the Lord in his ministry for the bringing in of the kingdom. They seem as deep-rooted as the everlasting hills and as imposing in their bulk. They block the way to accomplishment of desired ends. They shut out the vision ahead. They balk the disheartened worker with their grim assurance of immobility. They seem to laugh at his discomfiture and to mock his prayers. And, as the months and years pass and no change is seen in their contour, he comes often to accept them as a necessary evil and to modify his plans accordingly. Such mountains of difficulty loom up on every foreign field; each home district has its range with impassable serrated peaks towering ahead; few pastorates lack at least a "little hill." They are too varied in their nature to particularize, but they are genuine and heartbreaking hindrances.

Concerning all such, the Master has assured His servants that they need not continue as obstacles to the progress of His work. The question of their removal is one of authority. The command of faith is the divine means of removing them out of the way: "*Ye shall say unto this mountain, Be thou removed, and be thou cast into the sea; and it shall obey you.*" The question involved is *not that of an imposing faith, but that of an all-sufficient Name*. The worker has no power of himself to accomplish anything, but he is commissioned to wield the power of God. As he speaks to the mountain in the name of Christ, he puts his hand on the dynamic force that controls the universe; heavenly energy is released and his behest is obeyed.

Authority is not prayer, though the worker who prays can alone exercise authority. Moses cried unto God at the Red Sea (Exodus 14:15ff), beseeching Him to work on behalf of His people, only to receive the strong reproof, "Wherefore criest thou unto me? speak unto the children of Israel, that they go forward." And as he lifted his face in amazed protest because the way ahead was blocked by the impassable waves, Jehovah spoke again: "Lift thou up thy rod, and stretch out thine hand over the sea, *and divide it*" (14:16). As the impotent arm of the lawgiver held over the waters the symbol of the authority of God, there was immediate response. "And the children of Israel went into the midst of the sea upon the dry ground: and the waters [which seemed at first a barrier impossible to overcome] were a wall [of protection] unto them on their right hand, and on their left" (Exodus 14:22).

God delights to delegate His power to men, when He can find believing and obedient servants to accept and exercise it. So when mountains rise in their way, the Lord commands His disciples to speak unto them and bid them depart into the sea. He gives no instruction to pray, although that is understood. There is essentially the same charge as was given to Moses: "You have asked Me to work; I have granted your request, but I choose to do the work though you; speak to the obstacle before you in My name, and it will obey." As we obediently speak to the mountain before us, there may seem to be no immediate response. But as day by day we maintain the attitude of authority, knowing that we are commissioned to use the name of our Lord, there will come a trembling and a shaking and removing, and the mountain will slide from its base and disappear into the sea of forgetfulness.

God is endeavoring to train workers for a future and a mighty ministry of cooperation with His Son. He therefore has here and now conferred on them the privilege of sharing the authority with which Christ was endowed as the Son of Man. The burden of responsibility for its acceptance and its exercise lies with the individual believer.

The Binding of the Enemy

A fact that is anew being forced upon the consciousness of the Church of Christ is that a great and aggressive warfare is being waged against her by unseen and powerful foes. The Scriptures have long revealed it, but few have given this warfare the attention which it requires. "Our wrestling," the apostle warns us, "is not against flesh and blood, but against the principalities, against the powers, against the world-rulers of this darkness, against the spiritual hosts of wickedness in the heavenlies" (Ephesians 6:12, ASV). In the life of the Christian assembly, in the purity of its doctrine, in the fellowship of its members and in their individual bodies and circumstances, subtle forces are working with keen understanding and masterful direction. The opposition is veiled, but it is real, and it is sometimes tremendous. Because its source is unrecognized, it is the more effective. The powers of evil are allowed often to have practically free course in groups of believers. Troubles that might be easily overcome, if rightly diagnosed, are laid to other causes, and because the remedy is not applied, the difficulties may increase until the very existence of the congregation is threatened.

In one of the cities of Canada, the pastor of an Alliance church said to the writer, "There are about four different troubles going on all the time among my people. As soon as I get one straightened out, the devil has another ready to take its place." Answer was made, "Brother, you are right in your diagnosis of the source of your troubles, but you are wrong in your method of meeting them. What you are looking at are the coils of the old serpent through your congregation, and as you straighten out one kink, you may be sure that another will appear. Leave the coils alone, and go for the head; put your foot on that in the authority of the Lord; recognize the active agency of the enemy and conquer him; the coils will straighten out of themselves if he is dealt with." The same advice will apply in many other places. Let us learn the secret of victory through authority as well as through prayer, and our churches will come into the place of strength and be able to take the aggressive against the enemy.

We return to our starting point. The solution of every spiritual problem is to be found in the working of the divine energy. We long for its manifestation and pray with intensity and with desire that it may be released in our midst. Yet there seems often to be an unaccountable delay that perplexes and discourages. Are we fulfilling the conditions? God is ready to bless, but we fail to provide the channels along which alone can flow His supplies.

The Methods of the Lord

It is true also that the Lord is demanding a closer adherence to His appointed methods. As the individual believer matures in the Christian life, he often finds greater difficulty in maintaining spiritual victory. He had expected opposition to decrease, or at least to be more easily overcome. But he discovers that God is laying upon him heavier burdens and testing him for larger ministries. In like manner, as the age is advancing, the Church is being prepared for the final struggle by being taught lessons of individual responsibility that in the past were the property of advanced saints only. All believers might have known them, for they are revealed in the Word of God, but only the few pressed on to their attainment.

For the greater struggles of our day and the thickening atmosphere into which we are entering, the Church needs intercessors who have learned the secret of taking hold of the power of God and directing it against the strategic advances of the enemy. She needs those who have understanding of the times to know what ought to be done amid the crashing down of old standards and the introduction of that which is uncertain and untried.

God is waiting for those whom He can trust and use, who will have the discernment to foresee His steppings and the faith to command His power.

Authoritative intercessors are men and women whose eyes have been opened to the full knowledge of their place in Christ. To them the Word of God has become a battle chart on which is detailed the plan of campaign of the hosts of the Lord. They realize that they have been appointed by Him for the oversight of certain sections of the advance, and they have humbly accepted His commission. Deeply conscious of their own personal unworthiness and insufficiency, they yet believe God's statement concerning their identification with Christ in His throne power.

Increasingly they realize that heavenly responsibility rests upon them for the carrying forward of the warfare with which they have been charged. Their closet becomes a council chamber from which spiritual commands go forth concerning matters widely varied in character and separated in place. As they speak the word of command, God obeys. His delight is in such coworking. They have caught His thought concerning the method of the advance of His kingdom. Through them He finds it possible to carry forward purposes and to fulfill promises which have been long held back for lack—not of human laborers nor of financial means—but of understanding spiritual fellow laborers.

The Control of Personal Circumstances

In the varied presentations of divine grace and human experience which are set forth in the book of Psalms, two aspects embrace all others. The first is the *Messianic* where the psalmist, frequently in his own person, reveals the sufferings and the glory of the incarnate Son of God, whom he recognizes, however, only as the coming King of Israel. The second is the *individual* aspect, in which the relationship of the believing soul to God is portrayed in numerous phases. So fully is the human heart unveiled that David, to whom most of the psalms have been ascribed, has been spoken of by one writer as "not one man, but all mankind's epitome."

The inspiration of the Spirit of God was richly upon all the authors of the Psalms. Each of them knew God and loved Him with a passion that was, perhaps, not exceeded by any of the saints of the later dispensation. Out of their own knowledge of the inner life they wrote often more wisely than they realized. Without any straining of their words, it is possible to find foreshadowings of deep spiritual truths which in their full development could not be understood till Calvary had come and gone. Comprehension of the mysteries of the heavenly calling comes to men only as they are able to receive them. And, until the work of the cross was complete and the Holy Spirit was outpoured, even the most devout of God's true children were not ready for all that has since been revealed to the spiritual minds of the present age.

The Hunger of the Soul

In Psalms 42 and 43 is finely illustrated the thought which has just been stated. There is shown to us the awakening vision of a man whose heart was crying out for knowledge of and fellowship with

God. Desire was intensified by the fact that he was in exile. Who he was we may surmise, but his identity matters little. From the "land of Jordan," where the headwaters of that turbulent stream find their sources in the springs of the Hermons, he gazed with inward yearning toward the distant temple. At a former time it had been his privilege to join with the glad throngs of worshipers as they ascended the holy hill of Zion with songs of rejoicing and praise. Now, isolated amid the solitude of mountain fastnesses and cataracts, he listened with awe to one voice of nature calling unto another of the majesty of the Creator of all, while he himself seemed to be cut off from God and overwhelmed by the waves and billows of the never-resting sea of life.

It is sweet to note that, in his remembrance of Jerusalem, he was craving not so much for the ordinances of the sanctuary as for God Himself. It is a precious proof of the reality and the depth of his love that every opposing circumstance but increased his desire for the divine fellowship which he had once enjoyed, which to the pious Israelite found its center of manifestation in the place where God had chosen to reveal Himself. Though the sense of desolation was so great that it seemed to bear him down "as with a sword [a killing or crushing] in [his] bones" (Psalm 42:10), he still believed that the lovingkindness of the Lord was about him "in the daytime" to preserve him from the pursuit of his deadly foes. And then, when the shadows of night fell and the tabernacle of darkness enfolded him about, there stole into his heart the sweet strains of the songs of Zion mingled with his prayers to the God of his life, and he was soothed and comforted.

The Oppression of the Enemy

His complaint to God concerns spiritual rather than material foes. "Why go I mourning because of the oppression of the enemy?" he cries to the Most High, whom he accuses in his depression of having cast him off. The daily reproach of his opponents, "Where is thy God?" is an inward rather than outward voice, for he was far separated from those who would do harm to him. We are sometimes prone to think that the saints of Old Testament times possessed little clear conception of the powers of the unseen world. But this is a misapprehension on our part. It is true that in the book of Psalms the emphasis first appears to be laid upon visible and physical foes. Those the writer hates "with perfect hatred" (Psalm 139:22) because they were also the enemies of God. But we would be wrong in limiting the thought of the psalmist to what alone could be seen. It will be remembered that Satan is introduced in the very beginning of the Old Testament, and that he appears as the constant adversary of the people of the Lord. The facts also of possession by demons and contact with familiar spirits were well-known and often referred to with reprobation by the prophets and in the Law.

Furthermore, the book of Job was written long before the time of David and was unquestionably in his hands and those of the spiritual leaders of Israel. It was doubtless included among the Scriptures in which he meditated with great delight. In this remarkable narrative the veil of the invisible world has been drawn partly aside, and there is given a very startling view of the secret working of the great adversary who had been permitted to bring trouble upon God's champion. We see Satan so concealing his own working that the pious patriarch was actually deceived into believing that he had been set up as a mark for "the arrows of the Almighty" (Job 6:4). Knowing these facts as they did, it is not too much to claim that David and his fellow saints realized that at least many of the bitter persecutions which they suffered originated from the same dread source that was responsible for the afflictions of Job.

It is a common tendency in the present day to speak of every national calamity as "an act of God," when such should be laid, as surely as in the experience of the patriarch of Uz, at the door of the restless and malignant enemy of mankind. The permission of the Most High has been given, it is true, where such affect the Lord's people, and for this reason the writers of the Old Testament have a tendency to ascribe all things to the direct working of the divine hand. But there is, among the majority of the people of God, an inability to discern in their own sufferings what is the chastening of the Lord and what is due, in the words of the psalmist, to "the oppression of the enemy" (Psalm 42:9).

As a consequence, it is sad to see the numbers of earnest Christians, people like the psalmist with a heart for God, who are being beaten down to the ground and are unable to rise again. The roll of such is increasing, and it is incumbent on pastors and Christian teachers and workers to appreciate the reality of the danger and to meet the situation with a keen discernment of its source and determined will for victory. Unseen wolves are entering, "not sparing the flock" (Acts 20:29), and trained and fearless shepherds are needed who cannot only face the enemy with understanding and confidence and can deliver the prey out of his mouth, but who can also repair breaches in the wall of the fields.

6

The Victory of
the Believer's Countenance

Three times in Psalms 42 and 43 before us, there occurs a refrain in identical language. It varies somewhat in the Authorized Version where the translators have employed different words. In the first instance of its use (42:5), the last three words have been attached to the following verse, having probably been so arranged in some manuscript in order to remove what to some scribe seemed an abrupt transition of thought.

The following rendition applies in all three instances (42:5, 11; 43:5). It is quite literal:

Why art thou cast down, O my soul?
And why art thou disquieted in me?
Await God, for I shall yet praise him
—*The victory of my countenance*—and
   my God.

God is here revealed not merely as the Deliverer of the soul of the psalmist. In the existing circumstances of spiritual oppression and physical depression, that would have itself been a splendid achievement of faith. Jehovah is represented in a larger way, as the Giver of victory to the countenance of the psalmist, so that his enemies fled before his face. The Lord had endued His servant with His own authority from on high so that, as he went forward in the name of God, opposing circumstances should give way and spiritual enemies would flee apace.

This is a New Testament truth in an Old Testament setting. It is one with which every saved and sanctified believer should be familiar. The purpose of the Father provides that each child of His may be a sharer of the throne and the authority of His risen and exalted Son. Over all the power of the enemy this authority extends. It is the believer's right to bind and loose in the name of Him who has appointed him. As the psalm states it, God is Himself the Victory of the believer's countenance so that he fears neither man nor spirit nor opposing circumstance.

The Way of the Cross

It is the duty and privilege of every Christian to understand and enter into the divine desire for our perfecting and to claim the place with Christ, both in His cross and resurrection and ascension, that the Father has appointed. God has reckoned each believer in His Son to have died with Him at Calvary. "Know ye not," demands Paul (Romans 6:3ff), "that so many of us as were baptized into Jesus Christ were baptized into his death?" Alas, it is a truth of which very few who claim the saving grace of our Lord have any practical knowledge, but it is of vital importance. All of our growth into the stature of the risen Son of Man depends upon our identification with Him. "Our old man," the apostle goes on to say (6:6), "was crucified with him, that the body of sin might be annulled" (its power over us destroyed completely and forever). We enter into the experience of this through faith: "Likewise reckon ye also yourselves to be dead indeed unto sin, but alive unto God through Jesus Christ our Lord" (6:11). Then, as we positively present ourselves unto God as alive from the dead and withdraw our members from the demands of sin, we shall find ourselves through the action of the Holy Spirit, who carries out within us the action of faith, realizing the truth of the promise (6:14), "Sin shall not have dominion over you."

The way of the cross is the appointed path to the realization of the experimential sitting with Christ, which the Father has ordained for the believer. Our blessed Lord died at Calvary, and the bands of death being broken, He has been exalted to the right hand of the throne. There is no other way for the disciple than to be as his Lord. It is not a method of fleshly works of self-denial, but the firm belief that God does as He says, as we walk in the light of His truth. Our part is the simple entering by faith into that which has already happened at the cross, the tomb and the resurrection. We yield ourselves unto God that the Spirit may work in us that which He has revealed in His

Word as His divine purpose, a purpose which He can only fulfill as we abide in the faith that He is working in us to will and do of His good pleasure. We have died with Christ; we were buried with Him (not in the mere symbolism of water baptism, but in the apprehension of that work of the Spirit which baptism symbolizes); we were raised with Him in His resurrection out of that tomb in which all our sins and the old man, the root of all, were buried; and we have been made to sit with Him in the heavenlies, at the right hand of the Father. It is in the realization which this faith brings that we come to know that the Lord has Himself become the strength of our countenance as we see a new power working in us and through us in our ministry.

Practical Victory

The saint who has learned that the Lord Himself is the victory of his countenance confronts calmly and fearlessly whatever situation may arise, knowing that naught can prevail against the will that is linked with God. A firm and positive refusal that the enemy shall have any right to work in the life or the body or the circumstances will bring the foe to a standstill. And, as this attitude is maintained in quiet faith, a change will come, and the attacks will lose their force. However distressing the assaults, it is possible for faith to ask of his inner life, "Why art thou cast down, O my soul, and why art thou disquieted in me?" and to calm itself with the certain assurance, "Await God, for I shall yet praise him—the victory of my countenance—and my God."

The conflicts in our churches, in which neither

party will give way and which lower the spiritual power of the assembly, may be controlled by prayer and authority directed against those evil principalities and powers, whose working foments and continues the trouble. Individual lives, taken in the snare of the devil, depressed and hopeless, may be restored to their place of assurance, peace and joy in God. Attacks on physical health, on social relationships and on financial matters may often be traced to unseen workings and thus overcome in the name of the Lord.

In a wider outlook, the international tumults which threaten the ministry of the gospel through blocking access to needy fields and tying up the sources of financial support must also yield to the faith that directs the weapons of God against the satanic barriers. The countenance of Joshua was given such victory by the God of Israel that no man was able to stand before his face all the days of his life. Our wrestling, unlike that of Joshua, is not with the seven nations of Canaan, but their spiritual counterparts. These are the forces that are responsible for every opposing world issue. They, too, shall fall before the Church of Christ when her people, inspired and energized with a new vision of Calvary, shall rise in the name and authority of the Lord to refuse all interference with her world mission.

Princes with God

It was said of George Mueller of Bristol, in his later years, that he bore himself like a prince of God. So confident had his faith become through years of asking and receiving, so intimate was his communion with

God from uncounted hours spent in audience with Him, that his countenance and his whole bearing manifested the dignity of a member of the royal household of heaven. The society in which we move inevitably leaves its impress upon us. This is the more true when it demands the putting forth of our highest powers to walk worthily among its members, and when we further realize that it expects us in every situation to be an honor to it. We have been made through the ministry of our gracious Lord, "kings and priests unto his God and Father." If we believe this and walk in the conscious light of the Lord, there cannot fail in time to be seen in us what was said of the brethren of Gideon: "Each one resembled the children of a king" (Judges 8:18).

Victory over the Church's Foes

Among the spiritually significant stories of the Old Testament, there are none that contain deeper teaching for the individual overcomer and the whole militant Church of Christ than those of the outflow from the smitten rock at Rephidim and the ensuing battle with Amalek, recorded in Exodus 17. The lessons are so practical, they enter so deeply into the nature of the great conflict that is being fought in the heavenlies, they reveal so simply the technique of the warfare with our unseen foes, and they speak so confidently of complete and final victory that there is little left to be said on the subject. There are other incidents in the Word which deal with differing phases of the same subject, and all are of value. But this gives the most comprehensive outline of the spiritual struggle involved, and it closes with a statement of the eternal purpose of God regarding the cooperation of His people in securing present and final triumph.

Our Heavenly Possessions

Israel had come into a great and priceless possession. Out of the smitten rock, rivers of living water were flowing. They were a gift direct from the throne, abounding in life and blessing. They made possible the very existence of the people of Jehovah in the wilderness journey. The whole nation drank and was revived. There was no lack for either man or beast.

Rabbinical traditions speak of the streams following the host as it moved onward, the water flowing up the hills and down the valleys and gathering in pools at the places of encampment. To these traditions the apostle refers (1 Corinthians 10:4) when he speaks of the people drinking of "that spiritual Rock that followed them: and that Rock was Christ." In doing so, he does not give authority to the stories; his purpose is to direct attention to the second Person of the Trinity who accompanied the nation, providing for its every need and graciously protecting it in danger. The fact that a second time, toward the end of the wilderness wanderings, the rock was again smitten (Numbers 20) indicates the necessity for a further supply of water and reveals the falsity of the tradition.

For us there is a wealth of spiritual meaning in the record. "If any man thirst, let him come unto me, and drink" (John 7:37), the Lord still cries unto His people.

Christ at Calvary is the Smitten Rock of the New Testament Church. From His opened side flows the divine supply that satisfies every heart longing. So abundant is the fullness of the risen and living Lord, who dispenses that heavenly grace, that there is added to the invitation a wonderful promise: "He that believeth in me, . . . out of his belly [from the depths of his inner life] shall flow rivers of living water" (7:38). That is to say, the believer who abides at that Rock and drinks continually of its outpouring becomes himself a channel of blessing to other thirsty souls.

7

Victory over Spiritual Conflict

In the arid desert nothing is so vital as a supply of water. Sore conflicts frequently take place between the wandering tribes over the possession of a well or spring (see Genesis 26:18ff). It is not surprising, therefore, that the right of the people of Israel to the living streams of Rephidim was speedily contested. The fierce tribesmen of Amalek sought to drive them away, that they themselves might enjoy the abundance of this new oasis. Skilled warriors, trained in desert fighting, they were far more than a match for the recently liberated slaves of Pharaoh. Yet, untried as the Israelites were in warfare (Exodus 13:17), they must lay hold of spear and buckler and defend their heaven-bestowed blessings. The battle in itself was a hopeless one for Israel. Wherever divine interference lessened, as the weary hands of Moses drooped, "Amalek prevailed." There was no natural ability in Israel to conquer; their victory came alone through the power of that Spiritual Rock that followed them.

One of the hard lessons that must be learned by every seeker after the deeper life in Christ is that each new appropriation of heavenly grace and knowledge brings him often into a more subtle conflict. In the early stages of the Christian life, when abounding peace and joy have come in to fill the heart and the gladness of the Lord brightens all about him, his feet are "like hinds' feet," and he feels as if he were permanently established upon the spiritual "high places" (Habakkuk 3:19). But, ere long, he finds himself treading the Valley of Humiliation, where Apollyon must be faced, and passing thence to the dread experiences of the Valley of the Shadow of Death, where the evil ones press hard, temptation assails with crushing force and faith's contest with discouragement seems often a losing one.

Our Unseen Foes

As still further advancement in the knowledge of the Lord is given through the opening of the eyes of his understanding and he finds that he had been "blessed with every spiritual blessing in the heavenly places in Christ" (Ephesians 1:3) there comes the startling realization that the very heavenly places into which he has been introduced are the habitat of the powers of darkness. His acceptance of his seat with Christ Jesus (2:6), "far above all principality, and power, and might, and dominion" (1:21), provides him with authority and power for full victory so long as he maintains his place, wearing the defensive armor and wielding the offensive weapons. But, unless at this stage of progress, there is received clear instruction as to the divine provision for overcoming, he is liable to spend many months or even years of fruitless struggle and defeat.

Nor can any believer escape this conflict so long as he resolutely presses forward in the pursuit of true holiness and effective ministry. It is part of the training of the Lord's overcoming people. In the kingdom age, Christ has planned that they shall reign with Him from the heavenly places over the earth. It is consequently not strange that the principalities and powers who are to be dispossessed of the seats of authority now occupied by themselves should savagely resist their own displacement. These spiritual enemies oppose every forward step of the overcomer; they will seek to confuse his mind, sometimes drawing him into error or into extravagance in doctrine. They may even attack him in body, in circumstances or through his family or his friends.

This has been their method in every age, as illustrated in the march of the hosts of Israel toward the Promised Land. Among the children of Israel the powers of darkness subtly introduced "many foolish and hurtful lusts"; they sought to seduce them by the incoming of idolatry and fornication from the nations around; they incited them to murmuring and distrust of the providence of Jehovah; or they openly and fiercely attacked them, as through the Amalekites. In the same manner today, by both inward and outward means, "the wiles of the devil" are directed to the rendering fruitless of the life and service of the individual Christian and of the aggressive Church.

Many an earnest pastor weeps before the Lord because of coldness or disunion in his congregation. The successful evangelist is disturbed by some deadening influence creeping into the atmosphere of his meetings, by which his liberty of spirit is hampered, and by which souls are hindered from coming to the Savior. In many cases prayer does not seem to touch the difficulty, even when long continued. Nay, even prayer itself seems to be lifeless and God afar off. At times the enemy strikes back swiftly when some special effort is aimed against him. Workers break down, sickness weakens the frame, spiritual purpose slackens, and discouragement throws a pall of darkness that depresses every effort for the Lord. Such experiences are far from uncommon, as many will testify.

The Authority of the Rod

What is the significance of the rod as it appears in the ministry of Moses? The usual interpretation is that it symbolizes prayer. But there is no mention of prayer in the incident before us and in a somewhat similar case (Exodus 14:15ff.), the lawgiver is sharply told that the time is past for calling on God and that definite action is needed. There is a richer and more powerful meaning: *the rod symbolizes the authority of God committed to human hands*. By it the holder is made a co-ruler with his Lord, sharing His throne-power and reigning with Him.

It is a vision that staggers the faith of many. But it is a scriptural revelation of divine truth that is repeated in many places and in many forms. The overcoming saint is made a king and priest unto God (Revelation 1:6), that he may reign on the earth (5:10). He is given authority over the nations (2:26ff), cooperating with the risen Christ. He sits with the exalted Lord in the heavenly places (Ephesians 1:20), which is the center of the authority of the universe. In this position of privilege he is enthroned with Christ "far above all principality, and power, and might, and dominion, and every name that is named, not only in this age, but also in that which is to come" (1:21).

This is meant to be a present experience of faith, though its full development will be reached in the age which is before us. Let us not dishonor the Word of God that reveals these things by the unbelieving attitude that it means less than it has clearly stated.

All through the day "until the going down of the sun" (Exodus 17:12), Moses held out the rod over the valley in which Israel strove with Amalek. Was he praying? There is little doubt that his heart was lifted to God in unceasing supplication for the untrained soldiers of his people. But his holding out of the rod was a demonstration of the authority committed to him over the unseen forces which drove forward the Amalekites and which operate behind every battle (see Daniel 10:13, 20). Not in the visible but in the invisible lies the secret of success or failure. Over the spirit foes of Israel, which sought to thwart the purpose of God and to hold back His people from the land of their inheritance, Moses exercised the authority vested in him as the representative of Jehovah. By his sustained resistance to these mighty principalities and

powers, their ability to aid the Amalekites was nulli-
fied. And, as the sun went down, the beaten tribesmen
suddenly withdrew.

The principle holds in every conflict between the
people of God and their enemies. Where redeemed
man is concerned, the Father calls him into a ministry
of authority with His Son, the rightful Ruler of earth.
In the Old Testament some remarkable instances occur, such as that of Joshua at Ajalon (Joshua 10:12) or
that of Elijah (1 Kings 17:1) where the prophet boldly
declared that "there shall not be dew nor rain these
years, but *according to my word*." In those past ages,
however, the authority was limited to a few select
souls upon whom the Spirit came for special ministries. But the New Testament saints of the heavenly
places include all who are raised up with Christ and
who have accepted the death of the cross and the burial of the tomb, that they may attain unto the resurrection of which Paul speaks (Philippians 3:11). For them
there is a fellowship with the risen Christ in a larger
sense than others know. To them the powers of darkness yield wherever their authority is exerted.

The Hand upon the Throne

"Jehovah hath sworn," reads the Revised Version.
"Jehovah will have war with Amalek from generation
to generation" (Exodus 17:16). The first clause is not
correctly translated. "A hand is lifted up upon the
throne of Jehovah," the Hebrew reads. The lifting up
of the hand is a form of affirmation or oath, and from
this comes the rendering, "Jehovah hath sworn." The

meaning is to be found in the action of Moses. Lifting up his hand holding the rod, he took authority in the name of Jehovah over the foes of God's people. In his capacity as the representative of Jehovah he was exerting the authority of the throne when he lifted up his hand. It was a declaration of divine judgment to be executed upon Amalek and upon the demon powers who energized those cruel warriors in their enmity against Israel.

So, today, every consecrated hand that lifts the rod of the authority of the Lord against the unseen powers of darkness is directing the throne power of Christ against Satan and his hosts in a battle that will last until "the going down of the sun," that is, until life's day is ended. Paul prayed (Ephesians 1:17) that "the spirit of wisdom and revelation in the knowledge of him [Christ]" might be granted to the saints to whom he wrote. Thus would the eyes of their understanding be opened to see their full relationship to the risen and exalted Christ.

ENCOUNTER
WITH
DARKNESS

Foreword

While serving the publishing interests of his denomination, J.A. MacMillan also taught at Nyack College. For a number of years he taught a course in Principles of Missions. He considered some basic introduction to demonology as essential to missionary preparations. From his rich experience in China and the Philippines, he illustrated the nature and work of demons and how they are defeated through the finished work of Christ.

While working in Mindanao, MacMillan encountered widespread demon possession among the animistic tribes people of that region. The remarkable deliverance from possession in answer to prayer did much to promote the cause of Christ among these people. A strong growing church was born in the wake of that encounter with the power of darkness and the triumph of truth of Christ over them.

From his class lectures he began to write on the subject of demon possession. His initial efforts appeared as magazine articles.

Most of the material in *Encounter with Darkness* was first published in 1948 as a series of articles in *The Alliance Weekly*. Soon after, Christian Publications, Inc., published it in pamphlet form under the title *Modern Demon Possession* and it has been in print continuously since its first publication.

Though the writings of J.A. MacMillan are few, they have made a profound impact on the evangelical Church. His treatment of demon possession in modern times is still widely read by pastors, students and lay people. It is frequently cited in scholarly works on the subject of demonology. Merrill F. Unger includes at least four excerpts from MacMillan in his second book on demonology entitled, *Demons in the World Today*.

The increase of overt demon activity in Western countries calls for the enlightenment of the Church as to the biblical antidote to this spiritual plague. The widespread practice of astrology and the occult has produced oppression, obsession and actual demon possession in many people. The use of alcohol and drugs has, in some cases, resulted in severe demonic domination. Add to these problems the multiplication of false religious cults and you have a picture of the moral and spiritual decadence that has made possible an almost epidemic level of demon assault on human personalities.

Demon possession can no longer be left as an interesting academic consideration. Encounter with the powers of darkness is so real and so frequent that the Church must again practice the ministry of deliverance.

This new edition of *Modern Demon Possession*, now entitled *Encounter with Darkness*, contains additional materials gleaned from J.A. MacMillan's class lecture notes. The Foreword is also excerpted from his notes.

Introduction

Between the visible and material sphere in which human beings dwell, and that unseen and intangible spirit realm which surrounds and interpenetrates it, no veil exists save the inability of mankind to see the immaterial with eyes adapted only for the viewing of material things. Throughout this vast region, unseen intelligences—some good, some evil—everywhere move. With those that are evil the Christians believer has nothing whatever to do. He is to ignore them, save when they interfere with him; then his indicated duty is to resist them (James 4:7; 1 Peter 5:9; Ephesians 6:12). The appointed weapons of his warfare are the authority of the risen Lord (Mark 16:17; Luke 10:19) and the blood of the Lamb (Revelation 12:11). To the man of wholehearted consecration and of scriptural faith these will be found all-sufficient at all times.

On the other hand, the good angels have a constant and definite service to render to the saints of the Lord. They are called "ministering spirits, sent forth to minister for them who shall be heirs of salvation" (Hebrews 1:14). They are given charge over God's people to keep them in all their ways (Psalm 91:11). At rare times they may openly manifest themselves, even in these days. But the believer is never to seek contact with them, nor are his prayers under any circumstances to be directed to them. His knowledge of them, their service to him and their nature comes from the Word of God alone. To seek acquaintance with them is perilous, for in his present state even the saint is unable to discern between those who come to him from God and others who appear as "angels of light" (2 Corinthians 11:14-15), but in reality are spirits of darkness.

Divine wisdom has set bounds to the spirit world that may not be transgressed with impunity. Access to God alone, through Jesus Christ, is permitted. Human souls, conscious of ignorance and of need, and longing for heavenly help and fellowship, are given a hearty invitation to "come boldly unto the throne of grace, that [they] may obtain mercy, and find grace to help in time of need" (Hebrews 4:16). Such, however, must accept their place as sinners, and draw near through the atoning work of Calvary. The blood of the Lamb of God, slain in the divine purpose before the foundation of the world, furnishes the only access to the divine favor and fellowship. But the throne and the presence of the Eternal God is wide open to all who thus approach in sincerity and truth.

The Holy Scriptures set forth everything that God has been pleased to reveal of the other world and its inhabitants. To go beyond the limits which He has established constitutes disobedience that brings the certainty of His judgment upon the offender (1 Chronicles 10:13). There have been, nevertheless, individuals in every age who have recklessly disregarded the divine prohibition. With lawless desire they have sought to probe into the secrets of the prohibited spirit realm, and to communicate with beings of other orders than the human race. They have not realized that, whatever the measure of their intelligence, as compared with that of the spirits with whom they seek to communicate, they are at a profound disadvantage. The spirits which have been contacted—for such contact has actually and genuinely been accomplished—appear to know all about us, even at times to divine our thoughts and anticipate our actions. They can reveal or withdraw themselves at will, whereas we are entirely dependent for our knowledge of them upon their own statements, which have repeatedly been proven to be false.

From the human side, after more than six millennia of attempts at communication, there has been no authentic advance in knowledge. From whatever standpoint the subject be considered—whether wizardry, witchcraft, necromancy, divination, fortunetelling, consulting with familiar spirits, etc.—the gain had been altogether on the side of the spirits. Men and women have yielded themselves and their bodies freely and fully, losing health, mind, morality and their immortal souls. There is not a nation in which such intercourse has not taken place, nor is there any age that has not left records of it. Heathen priests have proven themselves to be adept in communicating with these spirits, often to a greater extent than mediums in our civilized countries.

Our study of this theme has been undertaken with a deep desire to help believers in Christ to avoid the pitfalls into which many earnest Christians have fallen. Ignorance and curiosity, resulting in deception and fear, have led numbers astray. Treading in forbidden paths, no matter what excuse may be assigned for the action, has brought multitudes into bondage from which untold suffering has resulted. Yet for all such there is deliverance. Not in psychiatry, through it has had at times a measure of success. But through the cleansing and loosing power of the blood of the Lamb (Revelation 12:11). We know of no other effective means.

1

Demon Possession

Some months ago the writer was asked by an Alliance pastor to come to his help. At once, accompanied by his wife, he set out for the home in question. On arrival, he found a small gathering of Christian friends who had been called for a like purpose. The cause of the meeting was the condition of a woman who had appealed for deliverance. Though not fully recognized at first, it was soon realized that she was under the power of demons.

The story of her possession was simple. A few years previously, following the death of her mother, she had sought the services of a spiritist medium, believing that she could thus come into touch with the departed loved one. The person in question was a sincere Christian but very poorly instructed in the Word of God. She had no conception that in thus tampering with necromancy she was breaking God's direct commands and also opening herself to the danger of spirit attack in some form.

The medium quickly recognized that her visitor was especially open to psychic impressions. Before long she asked her to unite with her in certain trance experiences and later sought her cooperation in her spiritistic seances, inducing her to surrender herself to the will of the spirits. Some time afterward, the woman found herself in serious trouble through the control exercised over her. But her efforts to obtain relief were thwarted both by the opposition of the medium and the active working of the demon powers to which she had yielded. In this condition several years passed before she sought the aid of the pastor above mentioned and made a full confession of her actions. There was still no realization of the sin, merely the desire to be free from the control exercised over her life.

Though the individual was in a coma, the scriptural test was at once put to the indwelling demon, "Thou evil spirit, has Jesus Christ come in the flesh?" (1 John 4:3). Instantly there came a response in the form of a bitter "no." The spirit being thus identified, another question was presented, "Spirit, what is your name?" Refusal to tell followed, but under the power of continued prayer, the name was eventually given.

However, there quickly came the consciousness that the demon was not alone but one of a company. All that night, from about 8 o'clock until 7 the following morning, the battle continued. In that time eigh-teen separate demons left the body of their victim, each one identifying himself before he left by uttering his name. Most of the names given were those of spiritual states, such as "Fear," "Death," etc. But these were varied by others, as "Chief," "Mug," "Legion," one calling himself "Chief Servant of Lucifer."

When morning came the patient seemed revived and normal, and it was thought by some that the work was done. Four days later, however, a hurried call came again, and a visit revealed the woman in the same condition. That night four more spirits revealed themselves and departed. For perhaps three weeks a measure of relief continued, and then the trouble recurred. The question arose as to whether other spirits had gained entrance, but this did not seem to be the case; rather there were those which had not revealed themselves. At intervals covering a period of two months fresh manifestations occurred, and these were dealt with as they appeared. In all, seven entire nights were thus spent.

The sufferer was throughout this time unable to take hold of the Lord for herself. Intense fear possessed her mind. At times, during the seasons when definite effort was being exerted by prayer and authority for the casting out of the evil spirits, she would come briefly out of the coma in which her senses were bound. In reply to exhortations to utter the name of Jesus or to give praise to God, she would attempt to do so, but immediately the spirits would seize her and use her hands in a fierce endeavor to strangle herself. Two brethren were constantly on the alert to hold her hands. At other times she would try to bite those about her, as a dog might do.

The trouble was seen toward the end of the long struggle to be attended by a sexual mania. One demon calling himself by the name of "Internal Masculinity Cacoethes" seemed to be the source of this uncleanness. He remained alone after perhaps thirty other demons had been expelled. Having gained a hold in the sensual part of the being, it seemed almost impossible to dislodge him. But God's Word gives unquestionable authority to His faithful people. "Ye are of God, little children," says the beloved disciple after his instructions regarding the presence and deceitfulness of the agents of the evil one, "and have overcome them: because greater is he that is in you, than he that is in the world" (1 John 4:4).

The end came at last. One demon, as we mentioned above, had held the fort defiantly, giving, whenever asked, the name mentioned above. On the last night the powers of evil seemed to fill the room. The patient, awakening from her coma, cried out in fear that spirits were coming at her first from one side and then from the other. These unseen beings were rebuked in the name of Jesus and seemed to withdraw. The quoting of passages from the Bible were resented by the indwelling demon with cries of "No! No!"

Finally a pastor said to the demon, "You are beaten," which he acknowledged, but refused to go. The spirit then said, "I will go out tomorrow." The reply was, "No, you will go out now." He spoke again, "I'm going out," and then, through the lips of the patient, "I'm outside now." At once the question was asked, "Why do you lie to us?" bringing the reply, "Because I am going to kill her before I go." Shortly after, in a sad voice the spirit said, "I must find a new home," and suddenly came out through the mouth, the woman nearly strangling. But immediately she began to praise God with complete freedom and has so continued. Attempts were made by the spirits to regain possession, but steadfast resistance has given full relief.

The terms "demon" and "spirit" are used interchangeably in the Gospels. Demons are a class of beings which are distinct from angels, a fact recognized by the Jews (see Acts 23:8-9). Their origin is not given in the Bible, and various theories are held regarding it. One certainty is that they are disembodied spirits and seek to embody themselves in human beings or even in the bodies of animals (Luke 8:32). They thereby are enabled to gratify sensual instincts—the grosser forms of which are intemperance and impurity—through the organs of their victims. Often a possessed person, though normally self-controlled, manifests strange appetites utterly unknown previously.

2

The Satanic System

Chapters 24-27 of the prophecy of Isaiah, although doubtless inspired by the conditions of the prophet's own times, refer to the coming day of the Lord. Thus we find a definite forecast of the overthrow of the satanic system in the beginning of the millennial period (24:21-23). Two great organizations are mentioned as subject to and undergoing the divine judgment. These are "the host of the high ones on high" and "the kings of the earth upon the earth." The first-named comprises the unseen "authority of the air" (Ephesians 2:2); the second looks forward, in its full development, to the world grouping of nations and their rulers at the end time, which we are witnessing today. With the latter group the present article is not concerned.

Probably the simplest scriptural division of the satanic system is given by the apostle Paul in Ephesians 6:12:

1. Under their great prince we have the "principalities," rulers of great world areas whose function and territories are suggested in the statement of the angel to Daniel (10:13, 20).

2. Associated with them are "powers." The two classes are linked together in more than one place, probably holding the relationship of prince and subordinate ruler.

3. "Rulers of the darkness of this world," a class of beings whose ministry is the keeping in darkness of the masses of mankind. From them doubtless proceed those cunningly devised heresies, such as evolution, which, backed by no genuine evidence, is yet accepted by the intelligentsia of our day, is defended with a pathetic loyalty and is forced upon the young in our schools as a reality.

4. "Spiritual wickedness in high places," an unnumbered army of demons who are the beings met with in the spiritist "seances," which are widespread throughout the country, gathering in multitudes to be deceived and fleeced.

Isaiah's reference to "the host of the high ones on high," speaks of "the powers of the air" (Ephesians 2:2), a body which is organized in fierce hostility to the purposes and the will of the Most High. Their organization is outlined in some detail in Scripture, so that a reasonably clear picture is given of it. At the head of it stands a fallen archangel of peculiar eminence and authority. He is called by a variety of titles, of which the most familiar are the following, grouped together in two places of the Word of God (Revelation 12:9; 20:2).

Satan's Titles

The Dragon. This appellation seems to be applied with reference to his relationship to the world kingdoms. Unseen, he works among and controls them by an unnumbered host of agents of varied ranks. He is not in any sense gifted with omnipresence but is enabled to travel with the speed of light from place to place. His authority over his subjects seems unquestioned, and his will is absolute where he exerts it. Occasionally we see evidences of his being, as for example in the insignia of the old empire of China where the symbol of the dragon appeared in every conceivable place. To us it seemed to be merely a figure of art, but to those who realized the extent to which that mighty nation was under the sway of idolatry and evil, the figure was a sinister one.

The Old Serpent. This term alludes to his ministry of deception of mankind in general and of individuals in particular. The prophet Isaiah foretells the deliverance from the spiritual blindness that is a universal condition among men. "He will destroy in this mountain the face of the covering cast over all people, and the vail that is spread over all nations" (Isaiah 25:7). The leaders of the world boast of the increasing light which is flooding over the world, and this is true of the advances made by science and by knowledge in general. But there is a widespread forgetfulness of God, so great that the nations of the earth are sitting in darkness and in the shadow of death. Our missionary enterprise is so futile, compared with the need, that the natural increase in population far outstrips the souls that are won out of heathenism. Thus the darkness is steadily increasing over the light, and heathenism grows mightily while Christianity is comparatively static.

The Devil. This title means the slanderer or the malignant accuser, an attitude he bears toward the children of God. The Scriptures present him as "the accuser of the brethren . . . which accused them before our God day and night" (Revelation 12:10). Truly the saints need a divine Advocate (1 John 2:1) to stand for them against this shrewd and diabolical enemy, who hates God and the people of God with an enmity that is undying. And the saints have a further protection in the blood shed on Calvary, for it is written: "They overcame him by the blood of the Lamb, and by the word of their testimony; and they loved not their lives unto the death" (Revelation 12:11). That "precious blood of Christ as of a lamb without blemish and without spot" (1 Peter 1:19) not only cleanses from sin but is the sinner's weapon against the enemy in his constant accusations and attacks.

Satan. This denotes the adversary of the believer, working through the multitude of principalities and powers, the world rulers of this darkness, the rulers of the darkness of this world (Ephesians 6:12), whom the child of God is exhorted to wrestle against and overcome as he wears the whole armor of God. There is an interesting word in Zechariah 3:1 descriptive of this evil opponent. We are told that, in a vision, the prophet saw "Joshua the high priest standing before the angel of Jehovah, and Satan standing at his right hand to be his adversary" (ASV). The old enemy was there to fulfill his agelong ministry of hindrance and opposition. But we read the strong vindication of the Angel of the Lord, "The LORD rebuke thee, O Satan" (3:2). From the authoritative rebuke of the Almighty, Satan must always flee. And it is ours to use the same rebuke as servants and fellow-servants of Christ and to know the same result. Principality and power, world ruler of the darkness, demon powers of the air—all must yield to us as we take our place with Christ in the heavenlies (Ephesians 2:4-6) and exercise the authority of His throne which He shares with His believing and obedient people.

Another set of titles is not grouped together but are used in varied places of the Word. One of these is "the prince of this world." Three times our Lord Himself used it of Satan.

The Prince of this World (John 12:31; 14:30; 16:11). This was a dignity conferred probably before his fall (Ezekiel 28:11-19). In the account of the temptation of our Lord (Luke 4:6), he claims the suzerainty of the kingdoms of the world in the presence of Christ, who does not deny his claim. Since Satan is the lord of earth's kingdoms, there can be no such thing as a Christian nation. Certainly kings and rulers may be Christians in their individual capacity, but the nations over which they are set do not acknowledge allegiance officially to God. (Instances of denial of such exist in Britain and America.)

The God of this Age (2 Corinthians 4:4). Satan seeks to supplant the true God in the hearts and the worship of mankind. Satan-worship is actually carried on in many places. The Yezidis of Iraq are devil worshipers, as well as others in heathen lands. But even in so-called Christian lands there are large numbers who definitely acknowledge Satan as God (for example, the "Lucifereans" of Paris; the cults of New York, Los Angeles, etc.; the attempts to secure children by some in New York).

The Prince of the Power of the Air (Ephesians 2:2). The seat of Satan is in the lowest of the heavens, possibly the atmosphere about us. Possibly Satan's sphere originally included the sun, which was out of action in Genesis 1. This is suggestive when we remember that idolatry has usually commenced with sun worship. Baal was the sun-god. It is significant that, whereas Baal means Lord when given by men, the Hebrew name for the sun is Shemesh, which means "servant." It is also noteworthy that the Scriptures speak of the heavens as not being clean in the sight of God (Job 15:15), and that the writer of Hebrews states that the heavenly things, of which the tabernacle and its parts and rites were but symbols, needed purification by the "better sacrifices" of the atoning blood (9:23). This was probably because of the rebellion of Satan.

3

Satanic Workings through the Ages

The Old Testament introduces us to a multiplicity of gods. We find mankind from the earliest times adoring its deities and yielding itself in varieties of methods to worship. The philosophies underlying these forms of worship were sometimes noble and lofty in theory, but in practice the trend was to become unspeakably vile. Among the more cultured nations of antiquity, such as the Greeks and the Romans, the Eleusinian and the Bacchanalian mysteries were such that the apostle to the Gentiles says of them, "Who being past feeling have given themselves over unto lasciviousness, to work all uncleanness with greediness," and again, "For it is a shame even to speak of those things which are done of them in secret" in the bosom of their societies (Ephesians 4:19; 5:12). And, in the latter part of the first chapter of his epistle to the Romans, he exemplifies his statement by outlining the descent from the knowledge of the true God to the indescribable abominations which characterize most of the heathen religions.

He speaks of three great steps downward:

1. We have the worship of idols, in which they "changed the glory of the incorruptible God into an image made like to corruptible man, and to birds, and fourfooted beasts, and creeping things" (Romans 1:23). "Wherefore God also *gave them up*" (1:24) to become like the idols they sought after, for that is ever the result and the curse of idolatry.

2. God *gave them up* (1:26) to descend below the level of the animals in the abominable crimes of sodomy and prostitution, bringing on themselves "that recompense of their error which was meet" (1:27)—the corruption of their moral natures combined with the evil diseases which follow immorality and cause the deterioration of their physical beings.

3. God *gave them up* (1:28 RV) "to a reprobate mind," a morally hopeless state, where the whole mind and nature become corrupted and depraved. Such is the downward path of heathenism wherever it exists, its devotees being devoid of moral truth and spiritual life. At times a desire for higher things may be traced, but there is not inward or inherent power to obey the upward impulse.

It is only, however, when we hear the same apostle declaring, "The things which the Gentiles sacrifice, they sacrifice to demons, and not to God" (1 Corinthians 10:20) that we realize the true source of the corruption. Behind every heathen idol lurks an evil spirit, and the foulness connected with idolatry springs from this root.

The heathen themselves know this to be the truth. They will confess readily that they worship not the image of wood or stone or metal, but the spirit which indwells it. Few indeed are the idols to which benevolent impulses are ascribed; the majority are feared and hated by those who worship. Often the gods are given hideous appearances that they may inspire greater dread in the fearful worshiper as to their nature. Such is the Chinese god of war, and the Hindu goddess Kali, the deity of destruction and death, with her protruding fangs and her necklace of skulls.

The worship of evil spirits, called generally animism, is frequently separated from visible and material representations of the objects of devotion. Demons may take as their abode huge old trees, rocks, caves, streams, etc., and cause the people to worship them there. What missionary has not come across altars reared at the foot of some ancient banyan tree, upon which sheaves of incense lifted smoky fingers in silent appeal to the dreaded spirits which inhabited it? Or, at the crossings of streams, inserted in the ground will be found a few spears of incense, renewed as one traveler after another seeks to propitiate the demon of the stream that he may be allowed to cross unmolested. Great is the fear of these water demons. We recall the case of an English sailor who fell into the West River at the city of Wuchow. No foreigner was near, and as the unfortunate man swam from sampan to sampan, trying to get help, he was pushed back into the water by superstitious natives until at last his strength was exhausted, and he sank to his death in the swift current of the river.

To the heathen the presence of evil spirits is a terrible reality. The fear of the supernatural rests like a pall over the day and night. Someone has compared the native to a restive horse, ready to shy immediately at whatever unusual occurs about him. He lives in continual dread, overcome by the belief that multitudes of demons are ever at hand to do him harm. In the most real sense his existence is under "the shadow of death." One African chief asked a missionary, "Bwana (white man), what do you think I look for each morning when I wake? It is, 'Who will try to kill me today?' I am always on the watch for someone who might do me harm." The devil is a murderer (John 8:44), and those under his dominion live ever in the dread of the unknown.

The fetishes that are common to many tribes and individuals are not gods but rather charms to protect them from the evils they fear. These fetishes are also, without doubt, indwelt by demon power. Some of them have the function of assisting the native in hunting or in trade or in securing a wife. A striking example is the "life fetish," compounded by the medicine man or witch doctor from the hair and fingernails of the individuals, combined with other substances. When made up, it is taken by the compounder and hidden away, perhaps in the dark jungle or at the bottom of a deep river. Thus the life of the owner is guaranteed, for it is hid in the fetish, and nobody knows its whereabouts. But how much safer is the refuge of the Christian believer, whose life "is hid with Christ in God" (Colossians 3:3), safe for time and for eternity.

When we turn to the Bible, we find it acknowledging the supernatural character of demonism in a number of passages. The Mosaic Law pronounced death against wizards and witches, not because their art was a mere pretense or imposture, but because it was a voluntary and real intercourse with evil spirits. The language of Scripture is too plain on this matter to be misunderstood. "There shall not be found among you any one . . . that useth divination, or an observer of times, or an enchanter, or a witch, or a charmer, or a consulter with familiar spirits, or a wizard, or a necromancer. For all that do these things are an abomination unto the LORD" (Deuteronomy 18:10-12). "Regard not them that have familiar spirits, neither seek after wizards, to be defiled by them: I am the LORD your God" (Leviticus 19:31). "The soul that turneth after such as have familiar spirits, and after wizards, to go a whoring after them, I will even set my face against that soul, and will cut him off from among his people" (Leviticus 20:6).

The case of King Saul is set forth as a solemn warning to all who would traffic in any manner with the supernatural (1 Samuel 28:3-25). We need not go into the sad story of the declension of the first king of Israel; he broke the commandments quoted above, with fatal results. It is recorded finally of him, "So Saul died for his transgression which he committed against the LORD, even against the word of the LORD, which he kept not, and also for asking counsel of one that had a familiar spirit, to inquire of it; And inquired not of the LORD: therefore he slew him, and turned the kingdom unto David the son of Jesse" (1 Chronicles 10:13-14). And Isaiah repeats the warning centuries afterward to the nation: "When they shall say unto you, Seek unto them that have familiar spirits, and unto wizards that peep, and that mutter: should not a people seek unto their God? for the living to the dead? To the law and to the testimony: if they speak not according to this word, it is because there is no light in them" (Isaiah 8:19-20). These direct statements and prohibitions of Scripture indicate that such practices and such practitioners were known to exist among the nations surrounding Israel, and that the chosen people were in danger of becoming contaminated by them.

The spiritism of our day does not differ materially from that of ancient times. The priests of heathendom are often expert mediums, skilled in intercourse with the spirits whom they serve. Their paraphernalia differs only in variety from that of the medium of civilized lands, and practically identical results are obtained from its use. Similar deceptions are seen in heathen "fortunetelling" to those which occur in Western spiritism. But it must never be forgotten that there is a body of genuine manifestations which have been borne witness to by reliable authorities in both West and East.

Since the advent of Christianity, the testimony of the early Church fathers proves conclusively that demonism continued to exist in the countries of the Roman Empire. Possession, apparently so common in the time of our Lord and His apostles, continued afterward, as is evidenced by the presence in the early

Church of a special class of laborers called "exorcists," whose duty it was to heal, instruct and prepare for admission to membership candidates for baptism who had been afflicted by "demons" or "evil spirits."

There is an interesting question as to the cause of the surprise and astonishment of the Jews at beholding our Lord cast out demons. It is held by some that this was inconsistent with their familiarity with the practice of exorcism and with the words of Christ Himself: "By whom do your children cast them out?" (Matthew 12:27). If, however, we examine carefully the Gospel narrative, the explanation of this seeming inconsistency will become apparent. For instance, we read in another place (Mark 1:27-28), "And they were all amazed, insomuch that they questioned among themselves, saying, What thing is this? what new doctrine is this? for with authority commandeth he even the unclean spirits, and they do obey him. And the report of him went out straightway everywhere into all the region of Galilee round about" (ASV). Similar language is recorded in other Gospels.

We read also in Matthew 9:33, "The multitudes marvelled, saying, It was never so seen in Israel." There can be little doubt that the wonder of the people was excited, not so much by the fact of the Master casting out demons, as by the manner of His doing so. It was "by authority," by "a word," or in the language of our Savior Himself, "with the finger of God" (Luke 11:20) or "by the Spirit of God" (Matthew 12:28). What amazed the Jews was the great contrast between the dread and apprehension with which their exorcists addressed the demons, together with their frequent failures, and the calm dignity and authority with which our Lord always spoke to them, an authority which was in every case at once acknowledged and obeyed.

There is another important passage of Scripture relating to this subject. The Revised Version renders the last petition of the Lord's Prayer, before the final ascription of praise, "deliver us from the evil one" (Matthew 6:13, Luke 11:4 margin). The same desire appears in Christ's final prayer for His disciples: "I pray not that thou shouldest take them out of the world, but that thou shouldest keep them from the evil one" (John 17:15). This rendering seems, from a careful study of the original, to give the correct meaning of our Lord's words. It reveals moreover the Savior's recognition of our present position and its danger. It makes most real the existence of those enemies whose attacks on us we are warned to resist (Ephesians 6:11). The "evil one"—through his hosts of malignant but intelligent agents—carries on a warfare in which there is "no discharge," but one in which we as reasonable beings are responsible to cast ourselves in earnest petition upon the care and the power of the Father in heaven for His keeping. Apart from such petition can we depend on being kept?

4

Who Are the Demons?

Who are these demons, which are everywhere distributed among mankind? Our knowledge of the unseen world does not permit us to state with assurance their origin. Scripture, while it speaks frequently of them, gives no definite information regarding whence they come. It details various orders of the angelic beings but tells little of their functions. That all are of God's creation goes without saying, for everything has come from His hand and was perfect when it was made. But we find now disorder prevailing in creation: there is but one source to which to trace it—the rebellion of Satan.

One-third of the heavenly angels seem to have followed the devil in his revolt against God (Revelation 12:4). Their number may be roughly estimated by comparison with those which remained faithful, who are spoken of as myriads of myriads and thousands of thousands (5:11). The passage reads literally, "Ten thousand times ten thousand, and thousands of thousands," which gives an incalculable host; one-third of this total gives the number which are rebellious among the angels.

There seem, however, to be others than angels who were involved in the mighty conspiracy of the devil and who have shared in his ruin: these are the demons. In the enumeration given by the apostle of the malign forces with whom the Christian has to wrestle, four classes are mentioned (Ephesians 6:12). The first of these are called "principalities," mighty satanic princes, who have been appointed by their dread master to rule over the nations. Two of such princes are indicated, the "prince of the kingdom of Persia" (Daniel 10:13) and the "prince of Grecia" (10:20). It would seem from this that earth's kingdoms are each presided over by one of these evil beings and that their councils of the nations are really dominated by unseen beings. It is a sad thought that Michael, the prince of Israel (12:1), is the only one among these principalities who remained faithful to God (10:21). We wonder sometimes at the confusion and lack of unity among the kings and rulers of the nations, but it is easily accounted for as we remember that these great unseen princes exercise the deciding influence among them.

The second class is named "powers" (*exousias*, authorities). We find them joined with "principalities" frequently (Romans 8:38; Ephesians 3:10; 6:12; Colossians 1:16; 2:15) but always in a secondary place, from which we judge that they are inferior in positions, probably as cabinet ministers associated in government.

The third class is called "the world rulers of this darkness" (RV). The name suggests a ministry of deception, the keeping in darkness of the minds of men, especially of the leaders of thought. To them is probably due the introduction into our educational systems of such heresies as evolution, to which men hold with strange tenacity, seeing there is no shred of evidence as to its correctness.

The fourth class consists of "hosts of wicked spirits in the heavenlies." The term "spirits" is used in the Gospels as synonymous with "demons" (Matthew 8:16; Luke 9:42; and other places). That the Jews recognized the difference between the classes of unseen beings is clear from Acts 23:8-9, where the controversy between Pharisees and Sadducees over Paul is mentioned. To these beings are due the gross sins and deceptions, the stirring up of the animal passions and the incitement to all sorts of sensuous and sensual passions. These are the beings that are present in spiritist seances, impersonating and deceiving people of keen intelligence, as the well-known leaders of the cults today.

These beings are also to the fore at religious meetings and are a source of peculiar danger, especially when the emotions are deeply stirred. Many earnest souls, who have been urged to entire surrender to God, open their beings with the utmost abandon to whatever spiritual power approached them, unaware of the peril of so doing. Such yielding frequently provides a channel for entrance of demons, who thus gain control of the will. To dislodge them and once more to free the victim is usually a most difficult task.

Their Probable Origin

As mentioned above, the Holy Scriptures refer frequently to demons without suggesting in any manner who they are. Let us be quite clear at the beginning of our study that they are not the spirits of the departed. Spiritists would have us believe that they are and that they can be recalled to communication with us almost any time desired. The demons themselves seek to emphasize this theory, that they may the more readily gain access to those who are anxious to come into touch with their departed loved ones. We recall a well-known Methodist minister in Toronto who claimed that he could communicate with his deceased wife, who would come to him in his study and with whom he would have at such times full freedom of communication. But the invariable end of such contact is the entangling of the seeker in the toils of demonism.

The demons who are contacted in the seance are wholly untrustworthy. They are described by such writers as Dr. A. Conan Doyle as malicious, liars, mischievous, unclean. Another writer, Dr. Hereward Carrington, connected with the Society for Psychical Research says, "I gained the distinct impression throughout the sitting that, instead of the spirit of the personage who claimed to be present, I was dealing with an exceedingly sly, cunning, tricky and deceitful intelligence, which threw out chance remarks, fishing guesses and shrewd inferences, leaving the sitter to pick these up and elaborate them, if he would. If anything could make me believe in the doctrine of evil and lying spirits, it would be the sitting with Mrs. Piper (the medium). I do not for one moment implicate the normal Mrs. Piper in this criticism." These spirits have no conception of truth, or desire for it. The writer, in casting out a demon, said in answer to some statement which it had made, "You are a liar, aren't you?" to which it replied cheerfully, "Oh, yes." Lying appeared to be its nature.

Demons must be carefully differentiated from the angels, whether the holy or the fallen. The demons, as stated above, are disembodied spirits, while the angels are clothed with spiritual bodies similar to those which the saints shall have after the resurrection. For we are told by our Lord (Luke 20:36) that the "children of the resurrection" are equal unto the angels (that is, those believers who are partakers of the first resurrection, Revelation 20:5). The inference is of course clear—that the angels are also equal to the children of the resurrection, having spiritual bodies.

Heathen mythology recognizes these demons and traces them to a previous golden age. But, if we realize that the ancient writers were under the inspiration of the "prince of this world" (John 12:31; 14:30; 16:11), it will be easy to understand that their words are what he would dictate. They are benefactors of mortal men, roving the earth and dispensing blessings and favors to them. If we recall that the heathen gods are demons who uttered oracles and received worship, we shall see how this doctrine of Satan spread widely over the earth, and how men were deceived into believing that these creatures were revealers of divine benefits.

5

Forms of Demon Approach

The approach of demons to individuals may be commonly classed in three ways: Oppression, obsession and possession.

"Oppression" is most frequently met with, though its source is not always recognized. Bodily sickness is often from this cause. The Apostle Peter (Acts 10:38) spoke of "how God anointed Jesus of Nazareth with the Holy Ghost and with power: who went about doing good, and healing all that were oppressed of the devil; for God was with him." If this passage be compared with the evening in Capernaum (Matthew 8:16), it will be noted that Christ's healing ministry there was twofold: "He cast out the spirits with his word, and healed all that were sick." But Peter classes all of the Lord's healing as the oppression of the devil, a fact that throws light upon the origin of at least some of the bodily and mental troubles from which our people suffer.

Under this head may be found many of the difficulties with which pastors are confronted. Spiritual and physical depression is often the direct result of the impact of spirits of evil upon the mind. Science has developed a method of dealing with such cases called psychiatry. But the psychiatrist is limited by the fact that he ignores as unscientific the actuality of the working of unseen powers, confining himself to natural causes. With his mental treatment also are often combined various forms of so-called shock treatment, the results of which are at times helpful though frequently not lasting.

Depression may result from the inward suggestion that sin has been committed for which forgiveness has not been obtained. In serious cases the sufferer may believe that he has been guilty of "the unpardonable sin," a hallucination that refutes itself, for if anyone has crossed "the deadline" of divine grace, there would be no inward concern about it. Conviction comes from the working of the Spirit of God, who in such a situation would have withdrawn from the heart and mind. Demons, who delight to torment their victims, cause often unbelievable anguish to those to whose consciences they have gained access.

Earnest Christians may be cast down by suggestions that they are personally failures. Pastors and workers are often inwardly accused that their work is not succeeding. Let the door be opened and credence given to such thoughts and there may follow a flood of petty charges within the soul which overwhelm the heart and break down the resistance. Apparently strong believers may be utterly cast down in spirit under such attacks. Faith is the spiritual weapon of the saint, but faith may be quite annulled for the time by believing the doubts injected into the mind by lying spirits. Often when the renewed human spirit seems steadfast toward God, a series of assaults may come on physical health, on financial or social circumstances or through friends, which puzzle the understanding; the questioning which may rise because of such things gives opportunity for the enemy to weaken the hold on the Lord.

Depression may take the form of unaccountable lowness of spirits long continued. There are those who never rise above a certain plane in their spiritual lives, like Mr. Fearing in *The Pilgrim's Progress*. But others of a more buoyant nature are often loud and constant in their attitude of praise. It is this latter class that are more seriously disturbed by a sudden loss of their gladness. We recently met with a brother who had for seven years thus suffered and who was greatly discouraged, not being able to discern the cause of his declension. Praise is one of the stimulants of the devout heart, and when the spring of joy is dammed it is hard to hold steadfastly on the way.

Fear is another induced attitude, more common than the majority realize. At times it may become intense and cause mental disturbance that is hard to allay. On the foreign field it may seem to be based on the surrounding conditions, but in the homeland it is usually a vague inward sense of impending trouble. The trouble is in itself, as a rule, imaginary, but it destroys the peace and holds back from the confidence and joy that are the right of the redeemed.

Oppression

Oppression is probably the most common form of the working of the enemy upon the human mind or body. The suffering caused may be largely imaginary, but the symptoms, on the other hand, may be very real. Cases have been seen on the foreign field where a physician's diagnosis has apparently revealed serious functional disorder, and the patient has been invalided at home. Yet when the home physician has examined the worker, no trace has been found of the indicated trouble. The change of environment has seemed to remove all signs of physical weakness. If we consider this to have any connection with the working of the enemy, it would appear as if there were oppression on the field which did not exist at home, the pressure being removed when the patient reached the homeland. This has occurred a limited number of times but often enough to be suggestive.

Depression is often the direct result of the impact of spirits of evil upon the mind. Many cases could be quoted, but one will be sufficient. A lady, about fifty years of age, was brought to a most deplorable state of nervous weakness. She was dealt with, first of all, regarding her spiritual condition and led to the Lord. Then it was pointed out to her that her condition was quite unnatural, that her nervous state was unnecessary, that it was due to pressure of the enemy upon her mind and that she could with the help of the Lord assert her will and throw off the power assailing her. In an hour she was the master of herself and has remained so for several years. The ladies who brought her were astounded and declared it to be a miracle.

Suggestion to the mind that the unpardonable sin has been committed is repeatedly the cause of mental depression. It can be pointed out to the patient that if that sin had been actually committed, there would be no conscience of it because the Holy Spirit would have withdrawn. When every other cause for depression has been explored, the teaching that it is the work of the enemy frequently clears up the situation. If the sufferer is rightly instructed on how to oppose and overcome the enemy, relief quickly comes.

The unreasonable pressure of fear is another most frequent difficulty. A lady sitting in a chair in her kitchen heard a voice telling her that she was shortly to die. A sudden fear gripped her mind, which quickly covered nearly every aspect of life. She stated that if she went down into the cellar, fear would possess her so that her heart would pound severely. A missionary among the Mohammedan people told how a spirit of fear came upon him until he would lie awake at night listening for murderers to come. These might seem to be natural, but they so overcame the individuals that their lives and work were hindered. An understanding of the cause of the trouble cleared away the dread. But in a thousand forms, this trouble is repeated, causing much distress and agony of mind.

A surprising number are met with whose ministry is disturbed by false guidance. They are not sure that the inward suggestions which come to them are of God, but they cannot determine what is right or what they ought to do. This indecision becomes a real burden to them and a decided hindrance in their service. A deaconess in a prominent church was seized with the conviction that she ought to confess some slight fault. At a prayer meeting of the members accordingly she rose and stated her failure openly. But at the next gathering the same pressure was on her mind, and she again confessed. Thereafter, at every meeting, there was a similar feeling of conviction; she did not confess, and the rebuke in her mind grew to such proportions that she was in agony of soul. When it was pointed out to her that the conviction was not of God but the act of an accusing spirit, there was quick relief with following complete liberty.

People of a sensitive nature often fall into the snare of believing that others about them are criticizing them. When two friends are seen talking together, the inference is that they themselves are the subject of conversation. This condition is more widely spread than is supposed; good friends are separated, bitter feelings are stirred up, false stories grow among believers for which there is no foundation. When the matter develops, it sometimes happens that sides are taken and that church rifts occur. A wise pastor can often gain spiritual control of such a situation by calling a few trusted members of like mind, and binding, by directed prayer, the powers of evil that lie behind the movement in his congregation. Every Christian minister should understand the subject of spiritual authority and should be prompt to apply his knowledge. Watchfulness and observation would prevent many forms of trouble which often split spiritual churches.

The Christian public is at times shocked by the news that some strong leader has succumbed to a nervous or mental collapse. It is discovered that for a period he has been suffering from unaccountable lowness of spirit. Others whose spiritual life is low find a fear growing upon them that they also may be overcome by the same trouble. Often the fact comes out that the leader in question has for a long time suffered from a belief that his ministry was not succeeding and that he himself was personally a failure. But to those closest to him, these things were far from the truth; however, they had observed in him a growing introversion and an apparent belief that his popularity was waning and that people were noticing his declension spiritually. He had begun to speak about giving up his ministry, telling his closest friend that he was a failure and that the consciousness of it was robbing him of sleep and peace of mind. Yet when this man was convinced that his depression of spirits, his fancied failure and loss of the esteem of his fellows were due to the suggestions of evil spirits—an idea he had never considered seriously—he was enabled to take fresh ground for his whole ministry, he began to oppose the spirits with definite affirmations of victory, and in a very short time he had regained more than he had lost for he now had a new viewpoint which was scriptural and convincing.

A young missionary lady in China, living with two companions in a river port, was suddenly seized with intense depression. So great was the effect upon her that the older missionary in charge sent word to the field chairman that she must be removed as she was causing harm at the station. Accordingly she was sent to the headquarters, where much prayer was offered for her without result save that her depression seemed to increase. The case came under the observation of the writer, who spoke strongly to her, saying, "Miss, you are doing wrong in keeping up this continued blueness of spirit; I want to tell you that all depression is of the devil." The words shocked her, as hitherto she had been petted and nursed with tenderness by all in the headquarters. She showed her resentment, which was a most hopeful sign. He repeated his words; pointed out that the Lord commands all of His followers to rejoice in Him; something she was disobeying. Then he indicated that her condition was due to her yielding to the lies of the enemy and that she must resist the devil. In a surprisingly short time she was back in her station, equipped this time to discern the attacks of the devil and to throw them off.

Attacks on Ministry

Who is there among Christian preachers who has not at times felt a deadness in the atmosphere of his meetings that seemed impossible to dissipate? Such may be overcome by prayer and an attitude of spiritual authority in the name of the Lord Jesus. For spirits of evil infest meetings where the truth is set forth, seeking to distract the minds of hearers and to resist the working of the Spirit of God.

The late Dr. Jaffray told the writer of an incident where, in circumstances of peculiar opposition, plans which were formulated in private meetings for prayer seemed to have been revealed in some mysterious way. Realizing that the enemy was responsible, the precaution was taken in each such meeting of binding the foe and of prayerfully covering each plan. The result was that the hindrances were overcome and success attended the work in place of frustration.

Our Lord, when teaching His disciples the principles of prayer, said, "Thou, when thou prayest, enter into thy closet, and when thou hast shut thy door, *pray*" (Matthew 6:6, emphasis added). How many of us have found that the closing of the closet door has failed to exclude the distractions which come. Prayer has at times been most difficult, concentration of thought seemingly impossible. Round about the heart and mind circle the unseen powers of the air, bent on checking the intercession and supplication of the prayer warrior. There is a remedy. Recognizing the source of the hindrance, quietly claim from God the clearing of the air of the closet and accept the divine working in quiet praise. It is quite possible to be freed from such foes and to wait on the Lord without distraction of mind or spirit.

The Believer's Authority

To the seventy who returned to Christ with joy (Luke 10:17,19, ASV), saying, "Lord, even the demons are subject unto us in thy name," the Master replied, "Behold, I have given you authority to tread upon serpents and scorpions, and over all the power of the enemy." Lest any argue that this authority was given to them in a special time and is not now operative, we will refer to Mark 16:17, ASV, the scope of which cannot be questioned: "These signs shall accompany them that believe; in my name shall they cast out demons," etc. All that went before is included in this commission and a wider range is given to it. "Them that believe" is the only limitation; he who believes and obeys has a wider ministry open to him than the vast majority of Christians have understood or exercised.

Yet, while the foregoing is true, it is equally true that not all are called or equipped for the full performance of what is here outlined. Nevertheless everyone who is named as a minster of the Lord and of the Word should examine himself as to whether he comes short of that to which he is commissioned. There are not a few serving congregations who are permitting conditions to exist among their people that are displeasing to the Head of the Church. There are others who face individual cases which need help and who realize that they are not instructed or ready for the task of deliverance.

The civilized world as at no other time in history, save perhaps during the period when the Son of God was on earth, faces a working of demon power. The advance of so-called Spiritualism witnesses to this. But, in addition, there is manifest in the very congregations of Christians great numbers who need special understanding and help. Our national educational systems show the influence of what the apostle calls "doctrines of demons." To meet these sad conditions every minister of Christ needs a more intensive knowledge of what the Bible has to say about the impact of the unseen world on the seen.

Obsession

In a Western city, at the close of the weekly prayer meeting, a young woman was brought to the pastor. Her face was sullen and downcast, and her whole appearance that of despair.

Sitting down beside her, the pastor asked, "Can I be of help to you?" Almost savagely came the reply, "I didn't ask you to speak to me."

"No," was the answer, "but it is easy to see you are in trouble. I am sure if you would open your heart we could find the cause of your distress."

She burst forth bitterly, "God has left me!"

The pastor said, "Why do you say that?"

With the same bitterness she answered, "I sinned against Him and He left me!"

The pastor said again, "My dear young woman, that is not God's way of doing. If anyone has told you that, or it has come from an inward suggestion, it is not true. His Word is, 'If we confess our sins, he is faithful and just to forgive us our sins, and to cleanse us from all unrighteousness!' He never breaks His Word. You are deceived by the enemy."

To this there was no reply, and the pastor went on, "Now, in your inmost heart would you not like to be back in the same relationship with the Lord that you were before this took place?"

Eagerly she cried, "Oh, yes."

He continued, "My dear child, you have been listening to the lies of the devil, and he has blinded your mind to the promised of the Lord. The very fact that you long to be restored proves this. If God had given you up, and withdrawn His Spirit, you would have no desire for Him."

In a few minutes she was on her knees praising God in restored fellowship. Her trouble, in the first place, had come from the seeking and receiving of subjective manifestations. When these had left her, and could not be regained, she accepted the devil's suggestion that God was grieved and had cast her away.

Obsession is a control of the human mind from without, similar in many ways to hypnotism. The direct cause of it is not always easy to trace, but it invariably is the result of having at some time believed a lie of the enemy. As a result the mind is blinded and the will comes increasingly under the control of unseen forces until the personality is quite swayed by them. There is despair and hopelessness. Usually, the individual fears that the unpardonable sin has been committed and that there is no possibility of again coming under the mercy of God. This fear, however, may also accompany other forms of mental distress.

The control of the will is the vital issue at this stage. But the will has become so influenced by false conceptions injected into the mind that it cannot respond to the presentation of the truth. In fact, there has been in some manner an unconscious surrender of the will which is not realized by the sufferer. Control must be regained before relief and peace can be restored.

Here again, the relief afforded by psychiatry is only partial, especially in the case of God's children. For where a truly regenerated person has been thus brought through deception under the power of the enemy, the renewed spirit can find no contact with God, yet it can be satisfied by nothing else. Quite recently a person who had been brought into a gracious state of spiritual liberty stated that she had undergone "shock treatments" in an institution, and that though apparently much better immediately afterward, the condition of mental and physical bondage sooner or later invariably returned. A firm grounding on the solid rock of the Word of God brought to her lasting assurance and renewed delight in witnessing for Jesus.

The objection is frequently made that a true child of God cannot be brought thus under the power of the enemy. Experience disproves this, for even spiritual believers and earnest and successful workers have suffered, some of them never coming to the place of complete deliverance. We have in mind a successful evangelist and Bible teacher who was affected in this manner and confined to a state hospital. His particular obsession regarded his own spiritual state, which he considered hopeless. He would converse on ordinary topics with clear judgment and maintained a remarkable grasp of the current questions of the day. His knowledge of the Bible was comprehensive, and he would not infrequently interrupt the visitor who read passages to him, quoting accurately from memory verses which followed. To the observer he seemed like an expert swordsman who knew the technique of spiritual swordplay but had laid aside his weapon and refused to use it. He would commend the visitor to the care of the Lord but could not be brought to pray for himself. He remembered the peaceful hours he once enjoyed and found their memory sweet, but felt he was out of the sphere of the Lord's mercy and died in this state of mind.

As mentioned above, the control and exercise of the will is the crucial point in deliverance. Two things are essential. First, faith must be stimulated to the point where hope awakens. Here the Word is the worker's main reliance, but it must be used in constant expectation of the enlightenment of the Holy Spirit in the mind that is being dealt with. The utter hopelessness of gaining a response from the bound human spirit by merely natural means is keenly felt in the contact with such cases. Second, the will must be given suggestive aid until it can function for itself. For the effort of the human will to lay hold upon and appropriate to its owner the promises and provisions of God's Word is absolutely vital. How can this be done?

In a very serious case of obsession, the individual concerned was a Christian worker on a foreign field. The mental distress was intense, including the fear of lost salvation. There was constant rebellion against her condition, though with so little hope that thoughts of self-destruction kept repeating. Strange statements came at times from her lips, as though suggested from some personality outside of herself. She was conscious of these, but her mind in such things was able to take no voluntary actions of its own.

The method adopted in deliverance aimed at the restoration of willpower, as well as the freeing of the spirit from the evil control under which it was suffering. Much united prayer was offered by fellow workers, but it was clearly realized that the sufferer must come to the place where she could exercise faith for herself and take a decisive stand against the powers that bound her.

Daily a brief session was held with the afflicted person. Fear of eternal loss was the prominent feature, and this was first dealt with. In order to quicken the will, the afflicted one was asked to make certain definite affirmations, setting forth positively the spiritual attitude which was desired. The worker said, "Sister, I wish you to repeat after me, 'I believe in the Lord Jesus Christ.'" This was pressed until a firm response came. She was then encouraged, "He that believeth on the Son hath eternal life. Claim eternal life."

The sessions were short, not more than twenty minutes daily, as there was much physical weakness. Step by step, each phase of the bondage of the mind was dealt with, until at the end the attitude was taken, "I resist the devil! I refuse the working of the devil!" At this point a deadlock seemed to arise. But, when the victim joined in the affirmation, relief came suddenly and completely. In less than two weeks there was a full resumption of service.

6

The Reality of Possession

Biblical Teaching on Demon Possession

To the mind of the Christian believer, no other evidence as to the reality of demon-possession is needed than what is recorded in the pages of the Word of God, and especially of the New Testament. There it is clearly stated that demon-possessed persons were frequently encountered by our Lord, and that He "cast out the spirits with his word" (Matthew 8:16), thus manifesting His complete authority over them. Men, women and children are depicted as being possessed; no class seemed to be exempt from the attacks of these evil beings. There were charlatans here and there, calling themselves exorcists, who claimed to be able to deliver people from the affliction (Acts 19:13), but their methods were poor and ineffective. Only the Lord Himself, and His disciples to whom He committed authority, could cast out the demons effectively. There is a possible exception, in the case of one man whom the disciples reported as doing so in the name of Christ and whom they would have forbidden because of jealousy for their own dignity. The manner in which he obtained his authority is not revealed, but that it was real the objections of the disciples confirm.

A number of instances narrated in the Gospels are connected with physical sickness. The lad at the foot of the Mount of Transfiguration is said to have been epileptic (Matthew 17:15), a disease frequently confounded with possession. It is also called a dumb spirit (Mark 9:17), while foaming at the mouth and grinding of the teeth are mentioned as other symptoms (9:18, 20). It is further stated that the spirit at times cast the boy into fire and water to destroy him. Luke adds no pertinent particulars but those mentioned are not uncommon in modern cases.

Our Lord, in delivering this boy, addressed the demon as "Thou dumb and deaf spirit. I command thee, come out of him, and enter no more into him" (9:25, ASV). This characteristic of dumbness is referred to several times (Matthew 9:32; 12:22; Luke 11:14). Other cases of deafness or blindness are mentioned where the influence of demons does not directly appear. But that these troubles are often the result of working of evil spirits in our day is undeniable. Various types of sickness may also be said to be due to this cause; in fact, the apostle Peter in one place speaks as if the great enemy were behind all physical ills. He said, "How God anointed Jesus of Nazareth with the Holy Ghost and with power: who went about doing good, *and healing all that were oppressed of the devil*; for God was with him"

(Acts 10:38). In the Gospels, demon possession and disease are spoken of as separate troubles. Matthew tells us of one evening when "they brought to him many that were possessed with demons; and he cast out the spirits with his word, and healed all that were sick" (8:16). Peter, however, groups together every form of ailment as the *oppression of the devil.* It would be well for those who seek divine healing to bear in mind the strong possibility that, behind the sickness with which they are troubled, there may lie the hidden working of the enemy. If we believed this, would we not always seek first the grace and power of the Lord, even when resorting to physicians?

By the majority of those who have given thought and study to this matter, the demons are believed to be a class of beings who are disembodied and who are uncomfortable because of their unclothed state. For this reason they seek entrance into bodies of human beings; or, if that be impossible, they do not hesitate to enter the bodies of lower animals. Still controlled by the physical desires which held them in the time when they were embodied, they can gratify these cravings only through the organs of their victims. This will explain the actions of many which are otherwise inexplicable at times. For example, a habitually sober person will become temporarily a drunkard under the control of a possessing spirit; a naturally temperate person may manifest gluttonous tendencies; a moral person may run to sexual excesses, etc.

This condition may be scripturally illustrated by the case of Dives, the "rich man" (Luke 16:24). Far-ing sumptuously every day during his lifetime, he had died and his soul had been taken to Hades, the abode of departed spirits. To "Father Abraham" he asserted that his tongue was parched to the point of torment, and he requested that Lazarus might be sent with water to cool it. But it will be remembered that his tongue was in the grave with his body; only his soul was suffering; yet every sensation of appetite pressed on him with intensity which he was unable to gratify. The demon, like Dives, has no physical organs and must become a parasite in the body of a living person, man or woman, in order to gratify his cravings.

Thus, in the case of the Gadarene demoniac, the expelled demons requested of our Lord permission to enter into the nearby herd of swine. Their hold upon the bodies of these animals was brief, however, as they probably vacated their swinish homes as the water was reached. A similar and well authenticated story is told of the late Ethan Allen, a minister whose ability in casting out demons was unquestioned. Having difficulty in delivering a woman from possession, he said to the demon, "You can go into my pig, if you will come out of this person." When he reached home, his wife at once told him, "Ethan, I don't know what has come over our pig." "Well, I know," replied Mr. Allen. "I told that demon he might go into my pig, but I didn't say he could stay there." And going to the pen where the pig was dashing itself frantically against the sides, he commanded the spirit to come out and was instantly obeyed.

We read in Luke 13:11-17 of the relief given to a

woman who was bowed down by a spirit of infirmity for eighteen years. Doubtless the trouble would be considered in these days a case of spinal curvature. But the spiritual discernment of our Lord at once detected the oppression of the devil in what seemed to her neighbors merely an unusual malady. He called her to come to the front of the assembly, where He sat teaching, and spoke to her words of comfort and authority, "Woman, thou art loosed from thine infirmity" (13:12). Then His gracious hands were laid upon her, perfectly restoring her to a normal carriage. To the objections of the ruler of the synagogue, the Master declared it to be a right and proper thing that a daughter of Abraham should be thus freed from the power of the enemy on the Sabbath day. Evidently quite a stir was created in the synagogue, the neighbors congratulating the relieved sufferer and rejoicing with her.

The demon expelled by Paul (Acts 16:16-18) was a fortunetelling spirit, common in those days, as also in our own. It is spoken of as "a spirit of Python," identifying it with the Roman god, Apollo Pythius, skilled in the pretense of revealing future events. The "sons of Sceva" (Acts 19:14) were professional exorcists who met probably with some success at times by their methods (see Matthew 12:27, "by whom do your sons cast them out?"). But when the demons were stirred to unusual activity, as they were by the revival in Ephesus, the crude working of these men proved impotent. The answer of the demon (for it was really the spirit who spoke), "Jesus I recognize, and Paul I know" (RV margin) reveals where the true authority lies, even in the risen Son of God. Those who know His name and walk in the faith of Him (Mark 16:17) have no difficulty concerning the personality and the power of the spirits of evil.

To enter upon an exhaustive study of the phenomena of demon possession would be too great a task in the space of this book. The subject is so broad in its ramifications that no volume yet issued has fully covered it. Through the ages past, the "mysteries" of pagan temples—Egyptian and Babylonian, Greek and Roman, Hindu and Chinese—have found their inspiration in demoniacal sources and their power to control their disciples in demoniacal manifestations. Today in heathen countries demonism is mixed in some form with the majority of religions. Taoism in China is definitely spiritistic; Lamaism in Tibet is, if anything, more so; India has its "devil-dancers" who are undoubtedly possessed. In the Philippines possession is common among some of the pagan tribes of Mindanao, and in other parts. One of the native preachers wrote to the present writer, just after he had left on furlough, that the *anitos* (medicine men) among the Manobo tribe had said to him, "Come to us, and we will show you greater miracles than your Jesus can do."

To pursue such a study is fascinating. Our purpose, however, is merely to indicate what is occurring in this land and to show the origin of the distress of many children of God who have unwittingly fallen into the snare of the devil. For it is a sad truth that Christians have not infrequently been deceived by the enemy.

Accepting falsehoods presented to them in various forms, they have suffered agonies of fear and doubt which need never have befallen them if they had been taught in the Word of God. The inspiring Spirit has given in the Word clear instructions as to the danger and how to avoid it as well as how to overcome the enemy in the event of his attacks. Truth is the heavenly armor of defense and also the heavenly weapon of offense at all times, but truth must be laid hold of and put into practice.

Upon pastors and evangelists rests the greatest measure of responsibility for the instruction of the flock of God. It is, in a special way, theirs to discern the signs of enemy-working and to deliver their people. It is theirs also to teach and to warn of the perils which threaten the spiritually minded. It must be realized that the "heavenlies," into which the saints are introduced by divine wisdom and grace, are in this present dispensation the habitat of "the power of the air." The believer who seeks the deepest experiences of the spiritual life may fall under deception unless he knows that Satan himself is transformed into an "angel of light" at times and that the archenemy is at home in religious gatherings where earnest leaders are "ignorant of his devices."

Full "abandonment to God," unless guarded by the knowledge of the methods by which the Spirit of God reveals Himself, may open the life to the invasion of spirits of darkness. This statement should be pondered carefully in desiring gifts and manifestation. The distribution of such is strictly the function of the Holy

Spirit, who divides "to each man severally [individually] as *He* will" (1 Corinthians 12:11, emphasis added). The seeking believer should have his eyes upon the throne, disregarding specific gifts (unless these are revealed as things which he should "covet" (1 Corinthians 12:31; 14:1). What the surrendered soul must pursue is the will of God as his chief and only aim, being watchful lest his mind be set on things which might promote carnality and be the issue of self-will. Many, many are the earnest souls who have unconsciously given themselves over through an unrecognized envy to grasp after what they have seen in the possession of others.

The Nature of Possession

Possession is the actual entering into the human body of one or more demons and the holding of the individual under their control. The renewed spirit may struggle against their indwelling, as is revealed by the strong convulsions spoken of frequently in the accounts in the Gospels. But freedom seems to be impossible to gain save through the intervention of a man of God armed with the authority of the Lord. Even then the demon will usually dispute the right of the servant of the Lord to interfere with him. We have heard demons whine, "I will not go; this is my home," when they realized that their hold was challenged.

The difference between possession and obsession is not always easy to discern. Demons will often seek to hide their presence, revealing it only when forced to do so. Usually the patient goes into a coma when the demon is in full control; in fact, that is the easiest form in which they can be dealt with. At such times the evil spirit will frequently speak in a voice which is easily recognizable from that of the one whom he indwells. Gruff masculine tones have been heard proceeding from the lips of a delicate woman, the presence of such voices being often a proof of possession when other signs are absent.

Some Demon Methods

As a rule, the possessed person is unable to speak the names of God or Christ. In like manner, prayer is frequently impossible. In the repetition of Scripture, part of the verse may be spoken until the divine Name is approached, then it is passed over, and also the pronouns which refer to the deity. Demons have been known to fear the quoting of Scripture and to cry, "No, no!" when it was used. They have used expressions of hate and threatening toward Christians who were active in seeking to cast them out.

Sometimes their resistance is most violent. An Alliance pastor told the writer of a case in his congregation. During the service of worship, a woman showed certain signs of possession. At once he left the pulpit and approached her, while an elder came from the other side. They laid hands on her, but immediately both were thrown to the floor in opposite directions. He warned against laying hands upon persons who were thus bound by the enemy.

Another pastor told of an elderly woman who was visiting at a certain church where communion was being administered. When the cup came to her, she said that something black came out of it and passed down her throat. This of course was a deception of the enemy, but from that time she insisted that she was possessed. Prayer and teaching from the Word would seem to relieve her for a time, but she would soon slip back into the same attitude, and full deliverance never came.

A young woman from a family in which the mother was a lifelong spiritist told the writers that she and her sister had seen a hand come down through the wooden ceiling of the kitchen and the ceiling break into flame, so that water had to be thrown on the fire to extinguish it. Dr. Nevius tells in his book, *Demon Possession and Allied Themes*, of spirits thus causing fires in China, but we have no personal knowledge of any similar case in this country.

In a singular instance, vouched for by the narrator, the possessed person was beaten by spirits until large black-and-blue spots appeared on the body, these not being caused by external blows.

A young woman with whom the writer was praying suddenly went into a coma. The enemy was rebuked, whereby she came at once to consciousness, but suffered intense pains, first in the heart and then in the spine. At each recurrence of pain the enemy was rebuked, and she was shortly completely free, after which she confessed tampering with spiritism.

The Entrance of Demons

How entrance is gained by the enemy is often difficult to trace. Where there has been contact with spiritism, through the Ouija board, the planchetta or through the attending of seances, the cause is of course manifest. Sometimes the indulging in lustful thoughts, caused not infrequently by suggestion to the mind by the enemy, gives an opening. It is a truth not always realized that any willful sin invites every other sin, and when some sin has been yielded to carelessly or thoughtlessly the sinner may find himself a little later beset with temptation that he may have thought had no appeal to him. Thus, when conscience is disobeyed, and known sin willfully given access to the mind and heart, the protection of truth is weakened or withdrawn and some spirit of evil may gain lodgment. The wearing of "the breastplate of righteousness"—not here the righteousness of the Lord, but the willing and doing of the Lord's will in that actions of the life—is a must for the Christian believer, as is also each other part of the heavenly panoply (Ephesians 6:14).

There are lives so poorly guarded by the will—for the human will commonly can hold the fortress of the life unless deception occurs—that demons expelled from one person may enter into another nearby. This is, however, rare in so-called Christian lands where the gospel is present in a measure of power.

What shall we say of the godly saints who in later life or—sometimes in early years of middle age—come under the power of the enemy? The question is a very difficult one, because it is impossible always to get complete facts. Often such have yielded to false suggestions as to their spiritual state. A favorite device of the enemy is to press on the mind the fear of having committed the unpardonable sin. Teaching regarding this question is much needed everywhere. But, let this conviction gain acceptance in the mind, and in the consequent spiritual terror the defense of faith is let down and the enemy presses in. So complete is human self-determination in the wise counsel of the Creator that God's people are responsible for standing against "the wiles of the devil." Provision is made for victory that is complete if the method of the heavenly Guide Book is followed. But in the pressure of shrewdly directed forces against the soul, confusion and dismay often overthrow the defenses. Apprehensive of demonic advantage or conscious of demon presence, the child of God thinks that grace has been withdrawn and he is delivered to the foe.

7

Modern Demon Possession

The record of demon possession did not appear first in the Word of God; communications with the unseen world have characterized the religious beliefs and practices of all nations from the very earliest times. These beliefs are in accord as to the existence and the working of superhuman intelligences in the midst of mankind. There has been at all times, and still is, much superstition mingled with human beliefs. But clearer light is steadily growing, and it is becoming possible to discern between the various forms of demon working that are seen among us, and to quietly and sanely dispossess the spirits which enter into the bodies of men and women, and to comfort the minds and allay the fears of those whose condition is less serious.

An important fact, but one much disputed among Christian students of this subject, is that believers may become possessed. It is urged that the Spirit of God cannot dwell in the same body with demons and that those who so suffer must of necessity be the unsaved. The belief is a natural one and has much to support it from the side of reason. Dealing, however, with actual cases of demon possession, where the evil spirits were in full control, the writer can testify that, however it may be explained, sincere Christians have been sufferers and have opposed and resisted the indwelling spirit, pleading the blood of the Lamb and calling on God for deliverance.

Possession may occur in many ways, and its onset is often most difficult to trace. Children are not infrequently victims of indwelling spirits (Mark 9:21); a number of cases have been brought to our attention where those who were quite young have shown every sign of being under demon control. In an older person, the history indicated that the condition had existed from the time she was about six or seven. How a child can come into this unfortunate situation can only be surmised.

Contact with spiritism, often in entire ignorance of the danger, is a frequent cause of possession. In one instance a Christian girl, whose mother to whom she was greatly attached had passed away, was told that it was possible to contact the spirit of the mother by means of a medium. Not aware of the evil of such approach, she was soon entangled in the mysteries of the seance. Before long the medium, realizing that the young woman had an unusual degree of psychic attainment, invited her to join her in the work of benefiting humanity in which she was herself engaged.

The invitation was accepted, and soon the young woman became, unwittingly to herself, quite under the power of the spirits.

Still unconscious of the fact that they controlled her, she entered a well-known Bible school. There, under spiritual influences, she began to realize that something was wrong with her. She confided in the wife of one of the faculty, and it was not long until her condition became known. At once steps were taken for deliverance. Over a period of three months some thirty-three demons were expelled, and she was delivered.

Another instance was encountered in the early part of 1950; the subject being a woman of about thirty-five. In her early childhood she had been cared for by her grandmother, who was a devotee of Christian Science and who also was interested in a number of the heterodox cults which flood America. As the child learned to read—she had a very precocious mind—she was used by the grandmother to read to her their literature. In this way her mind was prepared to receive demon working. For it is a most serious and solemn fact that, just as the Word of God is charged with heavenly power, so the writings of these cults convey to their readers a power that is diabolic.

The woman was converted when nineteen years of age but did not go deeply into spiritual things for a number of years; in fact not until she had begun to attend a Bible school. Then she began to seriously follow the Lord and was baptized. After this event, the spirits began to seriously trouble her. She had begun to help in the kitchen of the school where she was attending; suddenly, while working, she fell unconscious to the floor. This occurred a second time, whereupon she was taken to the hospital room. There the school doctor visited her and, as her actions were somewhat violent, decided that it would be best to commit her to the state hospital. A student who was interested in her asked the doctor if he would allow the writer to first see her, which was granted. She was partly unconscious, and a challenge being given to the demon, the response came from her lips in a decided "No." The demon was then commanded to name himself, to which he responded with the word "Cults." When this was followed by casting out of the spirits, the first group that left her called themselves by the name of well-known cults, surprising some of those present. At intervals, groups of demons were expelled, the number totaling 171.

A third instance was that of a young man of twenty-two years of age. He had been very desirous of the gift of tongues. Though warned of the serious danger of concentrating on any gift, rather than on the Giver, he persisted in seeking with intensity. Finally he obtained what he sought. So confident was he that the experience was of the Lord that he considered he now had sufficient light to carry him forward without the Word of God; the personal revelation was all satisfying. Then came suddenly the understanding that his tongues were not genuine. The effect was a most bitter disillusionment. He came to the writer's house, and while attempting to pray became unconscious. The test revealed the presence of demons, one of whom gave the name of "False Tongues." Deliverance came after a somewhat protracted struggle, and he is now free in spirit and mind and body. He has learned to abide in the Lord and is recognized as a helper of others.

These three recent cases were marked by symptoms very similar in character. The spirits would take entire control of the personality of their victim, causing the sufferer to become entirely unconscious. So complete was the coma that the individual was quite unaware of anything that had happened during the period of the attack, which sometimes lasted for as long as eighteen hours. During this time, the demons would respond to a test, would give their names, would try to talk with those about, at times would use obscene language or would threaten the helpers. When victory was finally given, and the man or woman was freed, there would be a period of a few days, or even two or three weeks, when the effort would be made by the spirits to regain the ground lost. This could only be thwarted by the personal resistance of the one who had been delivered, holding against the enemy the name and the blood of Jesus Christ.

Sometimes the afflicted person seemed to be able to see the spirits that surrounded him or her. This is usually a proof of possession; however, it is not always the case, as some, while conscious of the presence about them of the spirits, are unable to see them visibly. We have known some who claimed that they could see spirits accompanying them along the way they went.

Incidents of the appearance of dead friends, of spirit rapping, moving of tables and other objects are common phenomena. One woman, a preacher of the Assemblies of God, told of strange appearances in her home, where a number of spirits seemed to live, where serpents crawled on the floor and articles fell without apparent cause. When questioned as to who saw spirits, the reply was, "All our evangelists see them."

Three instances have been mentioned which are characteristic of one class of demon possession. But there are frequent cases where individuals do not become unconscious and where the spirit cannot be contacted by the means spoken of. It has been found impossible at times to deal with these, the spirit apparently paying no attention to prayers or commands, and this over extended periods. The individuals in such cases often claim to be conscious of the presence within them of other personalities, who they can at times call by name. It is impossible to judge such persons, as to their willingness to be delivered; they usually express real concern over their condition and desire to be relieved.

Another class of sufferers is similar to the above in that the spirits do not render them unconscious. Their experience of the presence of the enemy is usually that of deep mental or physical depression. A young man would complain of manifestations to his mind; at another time, he felt terrible pressure on his head and ears; again uncontrollable jerking would take control of his body. A young woman suffered from fear, from manifestations, from a strong desire for psychiatry.

These symptoms, apparently proceeding from demon power, were addressed as demons, called by name, and commanded to leave. There was no further trouble from these sources.

8

Demonology and Religion

Demons are behind all heathen gods and image
worship. The heathen does not worship the idol
but the spirit which indwells it. Everywhere in
heathendom this is encountered. Old trees are in many
cases supposed to be the home of demons; altars are at
their bases and incense smokes continually; some
mountains or hills are specially holy as the abode of
spirits; the banks of streams are often the resorts of
spirits, and the cross is marked by sheaves of incense;
the air is the abode of spirits, and in China high places
are crowned with pagodas for the control of the *fung-
shui* of the region.

Many of the religions can be traced directly to demon sources, their authors having been possessed to a
greater or lesser degree.

The religions of China are today corrupted greatly
from their original form. Confucianism and Mohammedanism have retained their first simplicity

more than the others, but their popular forms are altered notably. Confucianism, originally a system of ethics, has become mingled with idolatry and—with Buddhism and Taoism—is somewhat of a jumble in the minds of the common people.

Taoism is, however, recognized as a system of demonism. Originally it was a setting forth of the Tao, the Way or the Doctrine. Its originator was a philosopher, named Lao-tse, who lived before Confucius. The Taoist priest is in most cases nothing but an impostor who plays upon the superstitions. But he recognizes the existence of evil spirits and has a certain amount of influence through the worship which he secures for them. He also makes use of professional mediums. The priest writes a charm for the medium, who takes an incense stick in his or her hand and remains absolutely still, inviting the entrance of the spirit. The charm is burned, incense is offered, and the priest chants his incantations. After a time the spirit seems to descend upon the medium, who begins to tremble, and then announces which spirit has descended and asks what is desired of him or her. Whoever has requests to make takes incense sticks, worships and prostrates and asks for response concerning whatever matter is troubling him. Similar performances are carried on by gambling companies, who make a profit out of the performance. There is naturally much fraud. At fairs such things are often seen. Shrines are established, sacrifices offered and opportunities given for consulting the demon. People come from every quarter.

The *planchette* is also used. A pencil is attached to the branch of a willow tree. Two persons take hold of the branch which is forked, charms are burned, worship is offered, the pencil begins to move and to trace characters in the sand in a tray placed below. The *Ouija* board is a Western method of the same thing.

In Taoism and Spiritism we see not so much the efforts of spirits to possess men, but the desire of men to be possessed by spirits, and the yielding of their bodies to them voluntarily as their instruments.

A *medium* is a person who thus submits his or her body for the entrance of the evil spirit. When possession takes place, various manifestations may occur. The speaking appears to come from another personality distinct from the individual whose lips are being used. When consciousness returns to the medium there may be entire ignorance of what has been said.

What is known as *fung-shui* is met with in every part of China. It is closely connected with Taoism. The expression refers to the spirits of the air and the water, those who preside over those elements. Pagodas are built in elevated places for the control of these spirits. Lucky days, lucky spots for burial or for building, etc., are determined by the priests in accord with certain methods of testing the *fung-shui* of a district. Much of the local feeling manifested against innovations like the railroad, the telegraph, mining, etc., was due to the fear of these spirits.

That form of Buddhism in Tibet known as Lamaism, is peculiarly demonistic. William Christie, missionary to the Kansu-Tibetan border, told me that he has been at festivals where numbers of men and women come under the power of the demons and are strangely affected. Some jump up and down, others are shaken violently, some do themselves harm, some go into trances. He has seen several strong priests holding down by main force a man who was foaming. Some are simply hysterical and laugh and cry. Some speak messages, which may be rational or simply a jargon of tongues. A case in his knowledge was that of one woman, the wife of a Christian, who refused to submit herself to her father-in-law. He cursed her by the gods. Afterward, she would be often seized and thrown down violently while carrying water or doing other work. She died, and the man married another, who received the same curse, with the same results, and also died. Later, the Christian took a pagan wife, and forsook Christianity, when the trouble at once ceased.

Both in Japan and China there are notions concerning the superhuman power of the fox and the badger, which are supposed to possess people so that they are said to be "possessed by a fox."[1]

The devil dancers of southern India are said to be as truly possessed as was the man with the legion of demons in the days of Christ.

Fetishism and witchcraft are unquestionably connected with demon possession. It is true that in the case of witchcraft, by which alone about four million people are annually murdered, there is much deception and false accusations by the priests and witch doctors.

No country can be said to be free from these evil manifestations.

Other Cults

The founder of Christian Science (Mrs. Eddy) was subject to trances, and there is little doubt that this false cult is due to demonism. Mrs. White, the real founder of Seventh Day Adventism, received some of her revelations in trances. When one reads the weird ideas of Mormonism, Russellism (in *The Finished Mystery*), etc., there seems little difficulty in seeking for their origin in those "doctrines of demons," concerning which Paul warned Timothy.

Modern Spiritism

Spiritualism is not a correct term for the doctrines which are taught under its name. It is a philosophic term opposed to materialism. The correct name is Spiritism, which embraces the doctrine of spirits and the various practices which have grown up in the cult so called. Its central teaching is that the spirits of the dead can and do communicate and hold intercourse with the living. Because of this idea, the First World War gave a tremendous impetus to the cult, multitudes of people desiring to come again in touch with their departed loved ones who had died at the front. Outstanding men, such as Sir Oliver Lodge, the well-known scientist; Sir William Crookes, the greatest chemist of his day; Sir Conan Doyle, the novelist; William T. Stead, the journalist, and many others embraced the teachings and became exponents of them.

The rise of Spiritism in modern times can be traced to a meeting on the 31st of March, 1848, when a group of seventy or eighty persons assembled in the house of a farmer named Fox of Hydesville in the state of New York. They had come together for the purpose of investigating certain unaccountable rappings and disturbances in the sleeping room of Margaret and Kate Fox, girls of twelve and nine years of age. These children had devised a means of communication with the authors of the noises, who would reply by a correct number of raps to numerical questions and would answer other questions by a rap for an affirmative, and silence for a negative. The younger girl had also discovered that she could obtain a response to dumb signs, indicating that the spirit could see as well as hear.

Proceeding on this experience, the group elicited the following communication. The spirit claimed to be that of a peddler who had been murdered in the house five years previously by the tenant, a blacksmith named Bell, and that his remains were buried in the middle of the cellar. This information, on investigation, proved correct, and many others became interested. Other manifestations took place, and, as one said, "It soon became evident that an organized attempt was being made by the denizens of the spirit world to establish a method of communication with mankind." A suggestion was made that the alphabet be called out, and the unseen intelligences invited to respond to the letters and spell out sentences. This was greeted by a shower of raps, which was taken as indicating assent. Accordingly, the first sentence was received with quite a measure of awe. It read, "We are all your dear friends and relatives." A code was established for future communications.

It became clear soon that the power of communication was not confined to the Fox sisters and that other spirits were ready to communicate. The excitement became intense. So rapidly did the new doctrine spread that it was estimated in 1871, twenty-three years later, that the number of adherents had reached ten million. It crossed the Atlantic and reckoned its followers by myriads in England and the continent.

Some leading scientists have investigated the reality of spiritistic manifestations and have been convinced of their genuineness. Among these, in addition to the names above mentioned, are Professor Alfred Russel Wallace; Professor James, the most eminent of American psychologists; Professor Hyslop of Columbia University; Professor Abbott, professor of philosophy in Toronto University; Caesar Lombroso, the chief of the Paris police; Camille Flammarion, the great French astronomer, who said, "Any scientific man who declares spiritualistic phenomena to be impossible, is one who speaks without knowing what he is talking about."

The Phenomena of Spiritism

- Physical manifestations: Levitation or raising bodies into the air, moving tables, producing sounds, from a delicate tick to a heavy blow, passing articles through curtains and into closed rooms, etc.

- Chemical: Preserving from the effects of fire. A medium will take from the grate a red hot mass of coals in his hands without any unpleasant effect.

- Writing and drawing: A pencil will rise up and write messages by itself. A slate is laid on the table, writing is heard and messages are found on the under side. Drawings in colors are produced, the colors being found to be wet.

- Musical: All kinds of musical instruments are played without human agency appearing.

- Materialization: Human forms are seen, and these may be recognized by some as their departed ones. They can be talked with and touched. Garments and flowers materialize and dematerialize.

- Photography: Photographs have been taken of spirit forms.

- Automatic writing: The Ouija.

- Clairvoyance and clairaudience: Seeing and hearing at a distance.

- Speaking while in a trance.

- Healing: The medium heals by spirit power or diagnoses disease when in a trance state.

The Danger of the Cults

In First Timothy 4, the apostle Paul makes a clear and emphatic prophetic statement. He says, "Now the

Spirit speaketh expressly, that in the latter times"—during the closing part of the church age—"some shall depart from the faith, giving heed to seducing spirits, and doctrines of devils" (4:1). We have entered into these latter times and are seeing about us what the writer mentions. Numerous cults have arisen or have split off from the churches which hold to the fundamental truths of the Word of God.

These cults have departed from the faith and have given heed to seducing spirits and doctrines of demons. Drawn away from a full allegiance to the Word of the Living God, they have accepted human guesses, which have been enlarged into more or less elaborated doctrines. There is in many of them a foundation of scriptural truth, to which has been added a superstructure of human reason, which adds to or takes away from the divine original. This is what constitutes a "doctrine of demons"—divine truth attracting and giving confidence to the new disciple; but this truth is vitiated by skillfully propounded error. Multitudes have been drawn away, sincere seekers many of them, with desires after something deeper than they have received. Often these new disciples become more zealous than their teachers in the propagation of false teaching, as the power of the enemy gains control. Subtly and powerfully the mind becomes impregnated; earnest Christians being often deceived by the keen propaganda which presents darkness as light.

The literature of these cults is exceedingly dangerous. Just as the Word of God is charged with spiritual energy, and works on the heart with transforming power, so the literature of every cult contains satanic power that unconsciously influences the minds of readers, and quickly and quietly produces a deadness of the spiritual senses. The truth as it is in Jesus gradually loses its hold and is replaced by false ideas. The falsities of the cult, impressed on the hearer by repeated addresses, and by reading of the literature, gain a stranglehold on the mind, until only the Spirit of God can bring light once more to the darkened understanding. And this unfortunately, does not often take place; the disciple, wrought open by the power that underlies the teaching, becomes cocksure of himself, and is almost impossible to approach with pure doctrine.

The case cited in chapter 7 illustrates the inherent danger of reading cult literature. The person had been possessed from her childhood, and had apparently become infected by almost constant reading of the literature of a number of such heterodox bodies. Her grandmother, an ardent devotee, whose eyesight was failing, had used the child to read to her various books and pamphlets. When the demon was challenged, and had responded, thus giving indisputable evidence of his presence, he was asked to name himself, and immediately responded "Cults." Later, a succession of evil spirits came forth from their victim, each calling as its name that of some well-known cult.

We need not wonder about the connection of these cults with demonism. Their founders have been themselves demon-possessed persons and have been subject to spirit seizures. During these times the enemy has spoken his doctrines through them. In studying the lives of the founders of several of our modern cults, it will be observed that they were troubled with trances and visions in the beginnings of their ventures in religious leadership. Their teachings have been received from evil spirit sources, which is the cause most probably of their declension from the truth, and the acceptance of teachings which bear the mark of demon leadership.

Without commenting on the experiences of those who have more recently established such organizations, the history of Mohammed, the founder of the mighty sect which bears his name, is of interest. He became a sincere reformer and religious enthusiast. He retired for meditation and prayer to a lonely mountain. There a most vivid sense of the being of one Almighty God—Allah—entered his soul. At the same time some strange power descended on him, under the influence of which he would foam at the mouth and roar like a bull. To those in any way familiar with the action of evil spirits on the bodies and minds of men, there can be no doubt that these seizures were the work of demons. Less violent have been the reported actions of others, but the same result has followed—the origination of teachings which are contrary to the Bible.

The fact that such teachings are inspired by demons—of which there is no reasonable doubt, though they seem to be the product of human minds—means that the reader is unconsciously absorbing what is designed to influence him hellward. That it has this effect has been proven time and again by the gradual acceptance of what is contrary to the truth of God's Word. Untrue propositions are taken one after another into the mind and assimilated until the individual becomes a supporter of the cult and often a firmer one than older members. Almost invariably the final result is a turning away from the fundamental positions of the deity of Christ and His substitutionary atonement for sin to those of denial that He is the Son of God and of self-righteousness.

There is no safety for any believer except in an absolute acceptance of the inerrancy of God's Word. A doctrine that compromises in the slightest degree can be at once declared to be a "doctrine of demons" and should be turned from without delay. Apparent holiness of life is not to be accepted as a credential where there is the slightest departure from the divine standards. Subtle and shrewd are the methods of demons; after the slightest doubts are inserted into the mind, there is a swift but hidden following up of the advantage gained. Quickly, but unhurriedly, they pursue their advantage until the mind is under their control. Once this is gained, the recapture of the mind for truth is often practically impossible.

We have more than once seen persons of intelligence, who had begun to go forward in Christ, diverted to the following of some heterodox cult. Before long there came a complete loss of the heavenly vision and an absorption in the new teachings until nothing else could be spoken of. Views of the Bible were perverted and forced into channels which were strained and false. Desire for the salvation of souls was lost, the aim being to prove to others that the ideas now held were the ones which must be accepted. To make proselytes to these ideas all the powers were devoted. More and more the purpose of the gospel was lost sight of, and that which had taken its place became the objective of the soul. It need not be stated that God's salvation was no longer a thing to be sought after.

A keen spiritual writer has said:

> "May not these demons be the spirits of those who trod this earth in the flesh before the ruin described in the second verse of Genesis and who at the time of that great destruction were disembodied by God and left still under the power, and ultimately to share the fate, of the leader in whose sin they acquiesced? Certainly one often recorded fact seems to confirm such a theory for we read that the demons are continually seizing on the bodies of men and endeavoring to use them as their own. And may not this propensity indicate a wearisome lack of ease, a wandering unrest, arising from a sense of incompleteness; a longing to escape the intolerable condition of being unclothed—so intense that, if they can satisfy its cravings in no other way they will even enter into the filthy bodies of swine?" (See Matthew 8:31).

In every part of the world this tendency on the part of demons is seen, and everywhere demon possession exists. A missionary from the interior of Mindanao in the Philippine Islands stated to the writer that in the area where she labored almost every person had his or her controlling demon. Among the Taoists of China every device of modern spiritism is found; and the same is true in other lands where darkness prevails.

Note

1 John Nevius, *Demon Possession* (Grand Rapids, MI: Kregel Publications, n.d.), 104-105.

9

The Way of Deliverance

It is natural for men to fear the supernatural. In what is probably the oldest book of the Bible, Eliphaz speaks of the dread which came upon him (Job 4:14-15) in the presence of a spirit. Daniel (10:7-19) tells of the fear which fell upon himself and the men who were with him, so that they fled "quaking." Saul of Tarsus (Acts 26:14) gives a somewhat similar description of his contact with the Lord on the road to Damascus. John the Beloved (Revelation 1:17) fell at the feet of the risen Christ "as one dead." We may say that these appearances differ from the manifestations in our day. But such differences are only in degree— the mystery of the unseen world with its beings still brings a measure of terror on the hearts and minds of men, until familiarity has lessened the strangeness in the case of those who ignorantly press into the seeking of what the Scriptures forbid.

In the case of earnest servants of God, who know

His will and have come to an understanding of His Word, godly fear in His presence never degenerates into a careless familiarity as their knowledge and experience of Himself grows from more to more. Nor does there ever come an attitude of self-confidence in dealing with the invisible spirits of darkness, even though the consciousness of the authority of the Lord increases as they realize that "the spirits are subject" unto them (Luke 10:20). On the contrary, their apprehension of the stubborn subtlety of these evil beings intensifies, and they appreciate the fact that only on the ground of the blood of the Lamb is there any power to deal with them. But when faith with boldness lays hold of this appointed weapon, they find demons giving up their grip and surely, even though reluctantly, leaving their victims when commanded in the name of Jesus.

It is the will of God as revealed in His Word that those who are oppressed of the devil should be set free. The Lord Jesus came "to proclaim liberty to the captives, and the opening of the prison to them that are bound" (Isaiah 61:1; Luke 4:18). The era in which we are living is "the acceptable year of the Lord," and it will not terminate until the Son of Man comes again to proclaim "the day of vengeance of our God" and to shut up in the prison house of the "abyss" the rebel powers that have brought destruction and agelong suffering to our race. During this period of grace, Christ's servants are commissioned to "cast out devils" (Mark 16:17) as one of the "signs" which follow "them that believe." The inference is that throughout the age there will be the need for this important ministry. History and experience confirm this inference.

Qualifications for This Service

In the days of His flesh the Lord Jesus conferred on His disciples "power against unclean spirits, to cast them out" (Matthew 10:1; Luke 10:19, etc.). This was done by the impartation of a divine power which accompanied them as they went forth preaching the gospel of the kingdom. Sometimes they failed (Matthew 17:19), and this He told them was due to lack of faith proceeding from failure to exercise themselves in spiritual approach to God. On one occasion, at least, an individual seems to have taken on himself the work of casting out demons in the name of Jesus (Mark 9:38). The disciples would have forbidden him, but our Lord passed the matter over with the statement that the individual who was not against them (as the rulers and many others were) was on their part.

However, the epistle to the Ephesians (2:5-6) gives a wonderful breadth to the fact of the relationship of the Christian to his risen Lord. He is made alive with Christ through spiritual regeneration, raised up with Him in resurrection and made to sit with Him "in heavenly places" where Christ is enthroned at the right hand of God. The Apostle Paul thus anticipates the message of the Savior to the seven churches (Revelation 2-3), and sets forth the basis of the victorious life of the "overcomer," which so few Christians understand or seek to enter into. It is throughout an appropriation by faith of that which the Spirit reveals as ours in Christ Jesus. It is a present-day experience received through yieldedness to the cross. It is the acceptance of that identification with Christ which brings His "throne power" into the earthly ministry of the believer. It is a living "by the faith of the Son of God, who loved us and gave himself up for us" (Galatians 2:20). It is a practical exercising of the Lord's authority in matters which are met in His service. It is, moreover, workable and brings a blessing to the believer and to others who seek Him for help. Finally, it is all of God, "who hath reconciled us to himself by Jesus Christ, and hath given to us the ministry of reconciliation" (2 Corinthians 5:18) and also the ministry of liberation of men from the powers of the air.

Identifying the Enemy

The spirits of evil are quick to recognize those who are armed with the authority of the Lord and who have knowledge of their devices. From such they will often seek to hide themselves. At times they will seem to have withdrawn from their victim, when the time for dealing with them has come. Commands for their departure will bring no response, and prayer seemingly has no effect. The individual may have a period of apparent freedom and comfort, but it is deceptive. Or he will plead with the worker or workers to be let alone, control of the mind and will being held by the demons, although the possessed person seems to be expressing his own desire. Often the individual will profess willingness to unite in prayer or to join in singing or praise to God. But, almost invariably, if his assurance is accepted, there will be inability to take any spiritual stand.

The work of dispossession should always be preceded by prayer. If a group of believing persons can be gotten together to persevere in supplication, the result will be very helpful. Then, when the work of deliverance is taken up, the way has been prepared and the yielding of Satan's power is certain.

While demons will yield to the word of a single believer, when such a one knows how to use the name and authority of the risen Christ, it is well for two or three of like mind to work together. At times there may be struggling, when the power of the possessed person may seem superhuman. Or, at other times, the demons may cause the sufferer to attempt self-destruction, and it will be necessary to prevent this by force. Again, while one may undertake the exorcism of the spirits the others may pray either silently or aloud as the case may be. The united authority of the brethren will aid in the gaining of victory, although of course the power is entirely of God, and the ground of deliverance is the finished work of Calvary.

Full Deliverance

It must be remembered that in seeking the casting out of demons the worker is dealing with a crafty and lying foe. Not infrequently it may appear as if, in answer to the command to depart; the enemy has withdrawn, when he is merely in concealment. We have known of a sincere worker giving such a command and then asserting that the spirit had departed and the person was free when such was not the case. Shortly after the worker had left, the demon again manifested himself in triumph.

The possessing spirit may be of a very stubborn nature, and the work of freeing the sufferer may be protracted. At such times there may lie behind the difficulty some previous sin that gives a special hold. Impurity which has been practiced in the life may have given access to an impure spirit which holds to the ground gained with great persistence. Usually there will be some indication of this in the words of the victim or in the speeches of the demon if he be allowed to speak.

Demons may try at times to divert the worker by engaging him in conversation. In such a case it is well to silence him with some such statement, "We are not here to argue with you, but to cast you out. On the ground of the blood of the Lamb, we command you to go out of this body." On occasion the demon may become abusive and may threaten the worker. Or the sufferer, unconsciously to himself or herself, being under the complete control of the spirit, will endeavor to harm the worker, often snapping and biting like a dog or wild animal. Care must be exercised in such cases, and the worker's body kept under the covering of the power of the Lord.

When real deliverance is granted there will be no question about it. The freed sufferer, if a child of the Lord, will often praise Him with shouting and tears. Utterance of the name of the Lord, which may have been hindered previously, is now joyously free. However, the exhaustion of the body through the possession may be so extreme that for a period there must be rest and recuperation. In such cases prayer for healing and strengthening of the body will usually be needed.

After Deliverance

Our Lord Himself warned very solemnly of the danger of the life which has been delivered.

> The unclean spirit, when he is gone out of the man, passeth through waterless places, seeking rest, and findeth it not. Then he saith, I will return into my house whence I came out, and when he is come, he findeth it empty, swept and garnished. Then goeth he, and taketh with himself seven other spirits more evil than himself, and they enter in and dwell there; and the last state of that man becometh worse than the first. (Matthew 12:43-45, ASV)

This is a truth that needs impressing. If the life is left open to the world and its desires, there is constant danger of the return of the expelled enemy with reinforcements. Even in the case of the delivered believer, the peril exists. One of whom we have personal knowledge was pursued for weeks after deliverance by spirits of evil. They would come at night and try by arguments, threats and wheedling to find entrance. Discouraged at times, the restored child of God steadfastly resisted, and at last they withdrew completely, fulfilling the promise, "Resist the devil, and he will flee from you" (James 4:7).

The foregoing statements are all within the knowledge of the writer. The reality and possibility of children of God falling under the power of the enemy and finding themselves controlled by him is a tremendous reality. But it is also a condition that no one need come into. If the life has been regenerated through faith in and acceptance of the Lord Jesus, if it is surrendered to Him, if prayer and the reading of the Word of God is the daily rule, if obedience to God is sought after, there need be no fear. The Lord "is able to keep that which is committed unto him against that day" (2 Timothy 1:12).

The Power of Evil

Christian, dost thou see them
  On the holy ground,
How the powers of darkness
  Rage thy steps around?
Christian, up and smite them,
  Counting gain but loss;
In the strength that cometh
  By the holy cross

Christian, dost thou feel them,
  How they work within,
Striving, tempting, luring,
  Gooding into sin?
Christian, never tremble;
  Never be downcast;
Gird thee for the battle,
  Thou shalt win at last.

Christian, dost thou hear them,
  How they speak thee fair?
"Always fast and vigil,
  Always watch and prayer?"
Christian, answer boldly;
  "While I breathe, I pray!"
Peace shall follow battle.
  Right shall end in day.

Well I know thy trouble,
   O my servant true;
Thou art very weary,
   I was weary, too;
But that toil shall make thee
   Some day all Mine own.
And the end of sorrow
   Shall be near My throne.

   —St. Andrew of Crete
   (660-732)